Transfiguration Catechesis

A New Vision Based on the Liturgy and
the Catechism of the Catholic Church

Dominic F. Ashkar, PhD

Resource Publications, Inc.
San Jose, California

Nihil Obstat:
Reverend Isidore Dixon
Censor Deputatus

Imprimatur:
Most Reverend William E. Lori, STD
Vicar General for the Archdiocese of Washington

March 6, 1995

The nihil obstat and imprimatur are official declarations that a book or
pamphlet is free of doctrinal or moral error. No implication is
contained therein that those who have granted the nihil obstat and the
imprimatur agree with the content, opinions, or statements expressed.

Editorial director: Kenneth Guentert
Prepress manager: Elizabeth J. Asborno
Cover illustration by George F. Collopy
Author photo by Ghazarian Broummana

Reprint Department
Resource Publications, Inc.
160 E. Virginia Street #290
San Jose, CA 95112-5876

Library of Congress Cataloging in Publication Data
Ashkar, Dominic F., 1936-
    Transfiguration catechesis : a new vision based on the liturgy and
the Catechism of the Catholic Church / Dominic F. Ashkar.
        p.   cm.
    ISBN 0-89390-342-6 (pbk.)
    1. Catechetics—Catholic Church 2. Jesus Christ—Transfiguration.
3. Catholic Church—Maronite Rite—Liturgy. 4. Mystagogy—Catholic
Church. 5. Catholic Church. Catechismus Ecclesiae Catholicae.
6. Catholic Church—Liturgy. 7. Catholic Church—Doctrines. I. Title.
BX68.A84   1996
268—dc20   95-50111

Printed in the United States of America
00 99 98 97 96 | 5 4 3 2 1

To His Eminence Roger Cardinal Mahony,
a Prince of the Church

Contents

Acknowledgments

I should begin by thanking His Eminence Roger Cardinal Mahony, to whom this book is dedicated, whose remarks got rid of the doubts and fears I had regarding the decision to send this book for publication. I also express my sincere thanks and deep appreciation to His Eminence James Cardinal Hickey, who with open heart agreed to affix his imprimatur.

My sincere thanks also go to Archbishop Francis M. Zayek, Bishop of the Diocese of Saint Maron of Brooklyn, and the newly appointed Bishop John G. Chedid, Bishop of the new Diocese of Our Lady of Lebanon of Los Angeles, for their warm encouragement to publish this book. Thanks to Resource Publications, Inc., for their encouragement and their willingness to publish the book even before seeing the draft.

My thanks also go to Bishop Peter A. Rosazza, who took the time in spite of his busy schedule to read the draft, and to Msgr. Alan Detscher, Executive Director of the Secretariat of Liturgy of the NCCB, as well as Rev. Michael J. Cariglio, Jr., Pastor of Our Lady of Mount Carmel Parish in Youngstown, Ohio, a bi-ritual Maronite and Roman Rite priest; Deacon Joseph S. Nohra, also bi-ritual, who exercises his ministry at Saint Maron Parish and Our Lady of Lebanon Parish in Youngstown, Ohio; and Deacon George M. Khoury from Cleveland, Ohio, a lifelong teacher. They all took time to read the draft and evaluate it. They all have knowledge of both the Roman Rite and the Maronite Rite and are active in the pastoral field. I extend special thanks also to Patricia Kirby for typing, editing, and correcting with patience and tirelessness.

Grateful appreciation is extended to the following for permission to quote copyrighted material:

The Diocesan Liturgical Commission of the Diocese of Saint Maron, Brooklyn, New York.

Scripture selections taken from the *New American Bible*, Copyright © 1991, 1986, 1970 by the Confraternity of Christian Doctrine, Washington, DC 20017. Used with permission.

Excerpts from the English translation of Lectionary for Mass © 1969, 1981, International Committee on English in the Liturgy, Inc. (ICEL); excerpts from the English translation of The Roman Missal © 1973, ICEL; excerpts from the English translation of The Liturgy of the Hours © 1974, ICEL. All rights reserved.

Excerpts from the English translation of the *Catechism of the Catholic Church* for the United States of America Copyright © 1994, United States Catholic Conference Inc. — Libreria Editrice Vaticana. Used with permission.

Preface

On June 23, 1994, His Eminence Roger Cardinal Mahony of Los Angeles attended the ceremony of the establishment of the new Maronite Diocese of Our Lady of Lebanon of Los Angeles and the enthronement of its first Bishop John Chedid. Cardinal Mahony included among his remarks some comments about the Eastern churches in general and the Syriac Maronite Church in particular, from which I quote:

> I have always looked with great admiration to our brothers and sisters of the Eastern Rites, because you have been able to accomplish through your traditions something that has not been as well or easily accomplished in the Latin Rite. Through your deep understanding of mystery, and of the mystery of God's plan of salvation, you have kept alive in your liturgies, and in your prayers, and indeed in your rites a profound sense of the mystery of God. You have captured that sense of mystery in a way that unfortunately has eluded us as richly.

> I am so grateful to you for that wonderful gift to the whole church, and I just ask you to please continue to make that wonderful gift available to us, to keep reminding us in so many ways of the element of mystery.

In the Latin and Western Rite, we are more prompted to look for solutions, to designate plans, to create flow charts, and to do all kinds of things to try to live out our Catholic tradition. But you have been able to capture the essence of the *mystery* of redemption and salvation, and you have kept that sense of mystery alive in your liturgies, your symbols, your icons, your prayers, your hymns, and all that surrounds the Eastern Rites. I just thank you for that gift, and I urge you to continue to keep that sense of mystery alive for all of us.

Indeed, it is a sense of mystery that we in the Western and Latin Rite most desperately are trying to recapture today. It is sad for us in the Latin Rite to find many of our young Catholic Latin Rite members—especially young people—leaving to go to the Buddhists and other kinds of oriental rites. And why? Because they are looking for that sense of the mystery of God in our midst; and they want that mystery lived out in prayer, in liturgy, and in hymns.

And you, through your traditions, have been a splendid, splendid example of witness for that, and I thank you for that, and ask you to continue to teach us in the Latin and Western world the great pivotal central value of the mystery of God's presence in his plan of salvation.

You have also preserved in ways that the Western Rites are beginning to accomplish more fully. But that is also an understanding of the deep central place of Mary, as Mother of God, as Mother of the Church. Your whole sense of the tradition of the apostles and the saints, all of your prayers and liturgies, are constant reminders of that succession of saints, those men and women of heroic Christian discipleship who have been part of your traditions. You have continued to keep that very much alive. We again are grateful to you for raising up Mary in her proper role.

Our present Holy Father, Pope John Paul II, has deeply understood this. I think he has helped us in the Latin Rite to come to understand ever more fully that very special role of Mary as you have preserved it century after century.

Finally, you in the Maronite Rite have a long centuries-filled list of martyrs. Your sense of the cross of Jesus Christ, your understanding of the importance of finding and discovering the cross in our own lives, embracing that cross within the mystery of salvation and the ready availability of your Lebanese and Maronite people over the centuries to stand up for your faith, to be martyrs and to shed your blood for that faith, indeed is one of the proudest chapters in our Catholic Church history.

And that chapter is still being written in these days. In our own time, within the last few months, sadly we have seen further examples of Maronite Christian Catholics again giving their lives in testimony of the deep faith that is yours. Much of your martyrdom has enriched the church not only for your own rite but universally. And that sense of martyrdom has given great strength to all of us.

As we in this country, for example, may not face the same test of faith with respect to being martyrs and giving our blood, we indeed are continually being challenged and ever more so to be martyrs, that is, disciples who boldly and proudly and courageously live out our Catholic faith and proclaim all of the elements of that faith.

We will continue to face rejection and opposition and martyrdom in a different way. Our martyrdom here may not be through bullets and bombs and attacks. It is most likely to appear in newspaper editorials, in opinion pieces, in magazines, in newspapers, and in other such ways. But the strength to be faithful is still the same grace; and it

> is you, the Maronite Rite and Eastern Rite
> Catholics, who have so much history and
> experience to share with us and to teach us. And
> again for that we are very grateful to you....

After hearing Cardinal Mahony, I decided to dedicate this book to him, a Prince of the Church who speaks with the courage and the vision of a prophet of old. The mystery that Cardinal Mahony stressed is the mystery of the cross, the center of our Christian life, which was so well presented in the mystery of the transfiguration, giving the apostles a "foretaste" of the glorious cross and the courage to embrace the daily cross.

This book views the *Catechism of the Catholic Church* from Mount Tabor, the mountain of transfiguration, and presents it as a mystery, through the mystery of mysteries: the divine liturgy, mainly the Liturgy of the Word expressed in the Syriac Maronite Liturgy, the catechesis par excellence.

I dedicate this humble document to Cardinal Mahony with the hope that it will be the beginning of a long journey, the achievement of his dream and vision, and that it will lead many teachers and religious educators to the experience of their own mysterious transfiguration through the use of the *Catechism of the Catholic Church* as their guide.

Feast of the Transfiguration
August 6, 1994

Introduction

A story is told about a child who was playing in front of his house but little by little wandered off and became lost. So he did what small children are good at: he sat down and cried.

A man who felt some compassion toward the lad stopped to ask him what was the matter. The little boy told him that he was lost but could give neither an address nor a phone number. He could provide no clue that would lead him to the house. The man kept asking questions, hoping to return the child to his home, but he got nowhere.

Finally the little boy stopped crying, and as he looked around trying to find something familiar, he saw the tall church steeple at the top of which was a large cross. Then hope returned to his heart, and he told the man, "Sir, please take me to the cross, and I will find my home," because he lived next to the church.

For years, teachers and experts have been trying to lead children home, spiritually speaking, but in their attempts have been rather hesitant or even afraid to focus on the cross, the cross of suffering and the glorious cross. Yet we all know that if we are led to the cross, we will be home. That is the method Christ used during his transfiguration on Mount Tabor, giving his disciples, his students, a foretaste of the glory that could be achieved only through the cross.

The transfiguration event became the window through which the disciples realized and understood what Christ had been explaining to them: the plan of salvation that leads from the cross of the present to future glory. But this plan cannot be fulfilled unless we learn how to make of our present cross a glorious one and how to walk in his footsteps, coming down from the mountain instead of "building a tent" in which to rest comfortably, coming down to help, serve, and heal those in need.

A good way to express the relationship of the cross with the persons and the events of the transfiguration is to consider an antenna. What is an antenna for if not to give a clear message or picture? In order for waves, which travel horizontally, to reach viewers, a vertical instrument or wire must bring them down. Only then is a clear picture formed—only through the interaction of both the horizontal and the vertical. Our role as Christians is to be good antennae.

To take our analogy a little further, the best reception occurs when both the transmitting and the receiving antennae are perfectly aligned. The best reception occurs when interference is minimized.

This analogy can help us understand the events on the mountain top. Transmitted from above, transfiguration glory requires people who are perfectly receptive—disciples aligned with Christ—to bring down the signal to the horizontal or everyday level for retransmission to others hungry for salvation. Through the cross, Christ as well as his followers took and continue to take on the work of an antenna transmitting a clear picture of the plan of salvation, the possibility of attaining final glory through service to others.

This slight digression into electronics is a way to introduce the new *Catechism of the Catholic Church*. From the time it first came out, it has met criticism. But there are different reasons for the criticism, and not all the criticism is bad. Had there been no criticism, it might have meant there was little understanding of or attention to the catechism.

Then too, criticism can be constructive. When a message is spiritual and laden with mystery, it is sent with all the difficulties of a real radio or TV transmission, depending in large part on the terrain where the antennae are set up: to a specific people in a specific place, culture, and tradition. Even though the message finally reaches those for whom it is intended, it becomes ever less perfect and suffers interference. What a paradox that the very words and perspectives which allow us to grasp the message also prevent us so to some extent! The very message that might be clear and meaningful to an Easterner might be bizarre to a Westerner unfamiliar with Eastern tradition and culture.

We need to keep this in mind as we note the role that the *Catechism of the Catholic Church* intended for itself. The writers describe the *Catechism* in part as "an instrument for transmitting the essential and fundamental content of Catholic faith and morals" as "unchanging doctrine presented in the context of today's reality" and as "a point of reference for all who have the duty to catechize."

This is why I am sincere when I say that I would be more worried if there were no criticism of the *Catechism*. In our attempt to grapple with the human elements, the *Catechism* directly engages us.

The importance of human elements in expressing the invisible mysteries of God must be noted. This is especially true as regards the need for the cross as the way to glory, for we can see more clearly how these human elements can make God's message effective or ineffective, either clear and appealing or distracting and fuzzy.

My purpose in this book is to present the important elements of the *Catechism of the Catholic Church* from a different and simpler angle. Consider the fact that the feasts of the Transfiguration and the Triumph of the Cross coincide with the opening of our school year. If we were to focus on the coincidence of the two feasts at the beginning of our catechetical year, our Sunday celebrations could take on deeper meaning as we journey through the liturgical year.

These feasts are celebrated August 6 and September 14, respectively. These two months, while not the beginning of the Catholic liturgical year or the modern Western calendar, mark the beginning of the new school year. For young children, this time is in many ways even more important a new year experience than the "real" new year. So etched in memory is the experience of this time of year that when autumn comes, many adults in locales north of the equator feel a tinge of excitement they often associate with "back to school."

There is a metaphor in nature for the coincidence of these two feasts coming as they do at the close of what for most students is a glorious time of sun-filled, carefree vacation days. For those in the countryside, the harvest growing ever taller and then dying after yielding its fruits is a poignant reminder of the coming season. Even those in cities grasp the change from warm to chill, from gold to grey. In the air hang both dread and anticipation, anticipation made sweeter by autumn's pungent leaf fires and the belief that some day the seasons will change once more.

If we in catechesis were to join these two feasts with the beginning of the catechetical year and focus on their linkage, our Sunday celebrations could take on deeper meaning as we journey through the liturgical year. This change in catechetical focus would affect the celebration of our liturgies, in which the cross is frequently recalled and celebrated. What a wonderful opportunity this linkage offers to help children begin to grasp the message of the transformed cross and to live it from their earliest knowledge of the Lord. Tasting the glory of the transfiguration could help these young disciples through the many crosses they will face in childhood as well as later on.

The Korozooto of the ancient Syriac Maronite liturgy for the Second Sunday after the Holy Cross expresses a beautiful relationship of church and cross: "Thanksgiving to the Son of God. In his mercy, he established an unending river of life—his Church built on a rock and his cross over every church." A rock below and a cross above: providing this imagery and understanding of the church is how, in my opinion, we will lead our children to the cross that will lead them home. That is how we will help them understand it so they become like the little boy who recognized his home only in relation to the cross lifted high by his church. "Take me to the cross, and I will find my home."

This change in catechetical focus is my topic and my challenge to religious education teachers and writers. My purpose is not to create a new liturgical year or system but to find a more effective way, like Christ's, to present a valuable, much-needed message—one that has become almost lost among the many competing messages of our day.

The purpose of this book is to help good teachers become still better. It is directed to people of both the Eastern and the Western churches. It is for all who wish a taste of what it is to live as "sons and daughters of the Resurrection," in the words of the early Syriac Maronite Tradition, by becoming "liturgical people" who live the liturgical year around the paschal events.

This will be quite a challenge. It will require deep prayer in order to bring illumination and the foretaste of glory such as that of Jesus on the mountain of transfiguration. How natural for him to turn to his Father in prayer at the difficult moments of his life. The transfiguration followed on just such a time, as Jesus became more aware of his difficult mission. It was then that the resplendent light broke through and his Father's voice was heard. But first, the cross.

Do we have the courage to say with St. Paul, "I know one thing, Christ crucified"? If so, we can hope to become successful in our evangelization and catechesis like him, forgoing our reliance on sophisticated methods for the "folly of the cross."

Before beginning, I wish to make an important remark mainly to Western readers who are unfamiliar with the Eastern terminology, imagery, and ways of expressing faith. Texts written before many of the church councils use different terminology and vocabulary to which the Western ear and mind are not accustomed; they might, therefore, create a shock at first reading.

One

Catechetical Principles of the Transfiguration

The light of the transfiguration illuminates the cross so as to throw its message into clearer relief as the glorious antenna draws us forward, ever closer with each pulse of its transmission. There are lessons for the catechist as well as for the original disciples on Mount Tabor, where Jesus the teacher called his three friends for a unique lesson under the open skies. He called his students, but the call was not to remain on the heights. It was to return down the mountain to set up transmission facilities below to overcome poor reception or bring it to where antennae had never been set up. Some principles in this call were:

Called to Ascend

Called to a High Mountain

"Jesus led them up a high mountain..." (Mk 9:2): To be able to come into God's presence, we should be separated, or uprooted, from sin and the ways of the world. But that is not enough. Something else is needed: acceptance of the cross. But we, like Peter (Mt 16), are afraid of it.

Before his journey toward suffering, Jesus gave the three disciples a taste of glory. He took his three closest friends to the mountain. The disciples were called to see the manifestation of his paschal glory.

They remained there a while, as had earlier men called to the heights by God. When Moses saw God's glory, he remained on Mount Sinai for forty days and nights in the divine presence. Elijah also spent forty days and nights on his way to reach Mount Horeb, where God passed by him in a light breeze. Jesus' transfiguration crowned a period of forty days and nights following his fast; it was their focal point. Through the transfiguration, we—like the disciples—become acutely aware of our sinfulness and our nothingness, but the transfiguration also indicates to us the end of the paschal ascent: resurrection and glorification. Familiarity with the glory of the resurrection was the reason the disciples were called to the mountain. The transfiguration was, then, an event for the disciples more than for Jesus. But just what did they see? A Christ in deepest communication with his Father. A Christ at prayer.

Called to Pray

"While he was praying, his face changed in appearance and his clothes became dazzlingly white" (Lk 9:29). What happened to Jesus at that particular moment of the transfiguration cannot be really understood unless we have a minimal experience of prayer, for is it not in moments of intense prayer that we experience renewal and transformation with deep joy and peace? This security comes from "being with God."

Sometimes in a sacred place, we experience a transformation of our whole being. We may undergo external as well as internal transformation as our inner joy overflows. Through prayer we realize who we really are: the children of God. This must be what happened to Jesus. In his rapture, his humanity may have been transported to the point of sublimest union.

This is how the "dazzlingly white" quality of Jesus' clothing can be explained. Perhaps what happened was something like how the Shroud of Turin has been explained as becoming imprinted with Jesus' image: at the instant of his transport his outer garments were shot through with glory as if a divine camera shutter were tripped in the brilliant light. This radically altered appearance of Jesus was in fact so great after the resurrection that several times his followers could not recognize him until something else woke them up to the true reality.

Called to Be Part of God's Plan

"Suddenly Moses and Elijah appeared to them conversing with Jesus" (Mt 17:3). Moses and Elijah symbolize the Law and the prophets. These two major figures became the confirmation that Jesus would be the fulfillment of everything. The Jews had long believed that Elijah would return before the day of the Messiah. This event should have strengthened the disciples' faith in the shocking event to come: his passion. Did not Jesus use these very figures to explain to the two disciples on the road to Emmaus to help them see what seemed dark to them? "Beginning with Moses and the prophets he interpreted for them every passage of scripture which referred to him" (Lk 24:27).

The glory of the transfiguration was bestowed not only on Moses and Elijah, who appeared with Jesus, but also on the entire historical journey they represented. Present too at the transfiguration were all the righteous and just who suffered for glory, all those who served in the great functions of the People of God as prophets, priests and kings. In the person of Christ, the new Adam, a light brought full glory to all people from the first Adam onward. Rooted in the Old Covenant, the transfiguration also inaugurated the New. Peter, James, and John stood as symbols, alone with Moses and Elijah, the people of old. They all stood around the transfigured Christ and become one in the luminous cloud. They all announced the glory of the transfiguration, which is the mysterious inauguration of the kingdom of God on earth. It will continue in the journeying church.

St. James of Seroug, in his homily on "Moses' veil," said:

> In the mystery of his plans, the Father granted a
> spouse to his Only Son who was light...Moses
> appeared and traced with an expert's hand an
> image of the Bride and Groom that he
> immediately covered with a veil. He inscribed in
> his book that man will leave his mother and father
> and cling to his wife...The veil on the face of Moses
> has finally disappeared. Come all and see this
> splendor that we cannot stop admiring! The great
> mystery, until now hidden, is finally put in light.
> May the wedding guests enjoy the scene of the
> beauty of the Bride and Groom! The beauty of the
> Bride, until now hidden, has manifested itself and
> all nations admire her splendor. (Personal
> translation)

Like the disciples, we cannot believe in Jesus without being integrated in the history of salvation with God as its head. When we allow ourselves to be integrated in the ongoing flow, we then set out like Abraham, Moses, and Elijah on the journey of the People of God that he himself is leading. Just as this journey continues through history, so too the Word of God is not only past but also present. The stronger our faith becomes, the more pure of heart we become, and it is easier for us to see and praise God—"Blessed are the pure of heart, they shall see God."

Called to Be Sent Back Down

Sent to Become His Living Image

At the transfiguration, Jesus was intensely conscious that he is the beloved Son of God, the chosen one. Through the rays streaming out from the palpable unity between Son and

Father, we too, through the Son, become children and associates in this glorification.

We, his intimates, are invited to become participants in total confidence in the Father. If we stand in prayerful silence in his presence, we will be invited to enter into mysterious dialogue—not only with the one who will reveal himself to us but also with ourselves, because he is the only one who can bring us to ourselves.

To be human is to take on *someone's* image. We cannot exist by ourselves. To fully exist, we need to be recognized, appreciated, and supported by others. When affection, esteem, and admiration surround us, we feel encouraged to prove and affirm ourselves. But there is a risk, for when we begin expecting this "glory" from people, we become engaged in pursuit of an illusion. Human glory does not last. Only the glory that comes from God is lasting because we exist in God and we are created in God's image. It is this image we discover at the transfiguration.

As sons and daughters of God the Father, with Christ the Son we too are invited to enter into the cloud. This is the cloud of the "splendor of the resurrection." As we become attentive to the call of Jesus, above all responding to it, the cloud covers us and transforms us by his grace. Is this not the meaning of "communion": to receive the resurrected Christ?

Inside this cloud—through his light—gradually we discover who we are, the children of God who bear God's image. Here we come in touch with what is best in us. Such moments will protect us when temptation, confusion, and the material things of the world threaten to snare us.

Climbing the mountain with—and as—the intimate friends of Jesus should be an occasion of joy for us. We should not fear. It is an occasion of readiness to be sent, sent to proclaim the good news. It is an occasion to allow the Word to become flesh in us so others may see him in us. This is why we must be open to an eventual return from the heights.

Sent to Become His Living Antennae

Just as antennae are often placed on a mountain to transmit a clear picture to those who live below, so too the transfiguration event acted like an antenna on the heights. It was to broadcast the true identity of Jesus.

"Jesus came toward them and laying his hand on them, said, 'Get up! Do not be afraid.' When they looked up they did not see anyone but Jesus" (Mt 17:7-8).

From the mountain of glory, we are invited to go back down with Jesus to ordinary life, where soon he will have to face his darkest time of suffering and the scandal of the cross. Shortly afterward, his intimate friends will be left with this "foretaste of glory," this "prelude of paschal glory," echoed in the ascension and in the promise of his triumphant return at the end of time to strengthen and nourish their faith.

Is this brief encounter with glory not the story of our own faith, lasting just long enough to give us assurance? We can never capture and understand his great mystery. God will always remain this hidden Father who awaits the free love of his people. Like the disciples, we wish to stay up on the mountain but do not know what we are asking. It is much more difficult to recognize him at the foot of the mountain, in the plain, in the affairs of the world, where he is hardly recognized because of his ordinary, everyday appearance.

There, through our response to the call of God, through our daily round of worldly duties and events, we receive a clear image of the continually broadcast transfiguration experience. Turned toward the transmission site where our antennae are anchored, we are able to transmit a clear picture onto the screen of everyday life.

Sent to Become a Consuming Flame

Our return to everyday affairs is not a simple descent as of tourists after a pleasant trip. The descent from the transfiguration is one that continues to hold and consume us in its white-hot heat. Mary's own transfiguration event at the angel's message mirrors this, as the Maronite Liturgy of the Feast of the Annunciation so poignantly presents her reaction:

> The Angel said, "Mary, the power of God's Spirit is now upon you. Your son is the long-awaited hope of the prophets. He dwells in eternal realms, and fiery ranks of angels accompany him, for he is the flaming Word of God, a searing fire, a white hot coal." Mary said, "I am a mortal creature. Surely I will be consumed by God's all-consuming fire. How fearful is this moment! How my breath leaves me for fear! How humble am I, and how overcome that such a thing should come to pass! (Hoosoyo, Prayer of Forgiveness, Sunday of the Annunciation to Mary).

Mary, like Moses and Elijah and all the host of prophets, felt God's searing fire that consumes those who contemplate it. A vision of the glorious flame accompanied their entry into a deep covenant with God and people, for God calls us so that he can send us to find his image in others. This was the call for Mary his mother when from the cross Jesus said: "Woman, there is your son" (Jn 19:26). As Mary would find her son in his family of faith, so too are we called to recognize him in all her other sons and daughters. This was also his message to Mary Magdalene after his resurrection, "Do not cling to me, for I have not yet ascended to the Father. Rather, go to my brothers, and tell them..." (Jn 20:17). This was his message to his disciples of Emmaus, too. When they recognized him, they went back to Jerusalem to the brethren (Lk 24:33), for had he not instructed them to "go, therefore, and make disciples of all nations" (Mt 28:19)?

So too Christ wants to send us to bring back the lost glory to the world and its people who have separated themselves from it. His purpose in this mission is to bring back his glory to the heart of humanity. He sends us so that the transfiguration may become a continual event. We who have seen his glory no longer must be silent as he instructed his disciples on Mount Tabor: "Do not tell anyone of the vision until the Son of Man rises from the dead" (Mt 17:9).

That day has come for Christ but also for ourselves. How can this flame we received remain without inflaming our hearts and those of others?

Sent on a Journey

For us who journey in faith, the transfiguration, the communion of Jesus with the Father and the Spirit, will always be a mystery not totally understood until the end of the journey, when we are fully assumed in glorious communion with the Trinity. Transfiguration will be the moment of fulfillment in total harmony with ourselves, others, and the world.

Until that day, we make a lifelong journey toward transfiguration. From the beginning of our journey, we possess the taste of glory. The journeying church is fed, sustained, and supported by nourishment that brings us once again into transforming encounter with Christ: the sacraments, as they are called in the Western Church, or the mysteries, as they are called in the Eastern Church. The mysteries or sacraments of initiation—baptism, confirmation/chrismation, and Eucharist—mark us with the seal of transfiguration and communicate to us, the church, the glory of the resurrected and transfigured Christ.

The other four sacraments or mysteries change our spiritual personalities. Marriage or crowning is an image of the transfiguration that Christ gave his church at Cana when he changed water into wine. Holy orders—priesthood—is a vocation to transfigure the world by divinizing it. Reconciliation or penance restores us from our brokenness with God. The anointing of the sick transfigures weakness into strength and suffering into glory.

As God touches human events, so he also touches things of this world that can be used to transfigure the world in which we journey—the sacramentals. These have the same purpose as the sacraments or mysteries: to transfigure the world.

Transfiguration, then, is not only a spiritual but also a physical effort because the transfiguration process is in the soul of the believer who journeys in this earthly life. The transfiguration process will find its fulfillment at the Parousia, when the Lord will return the kingdom to the Father and when the church, born of the Trinity and united to the whole creation, will be perfectly reintegrated into the mystery of the Trinity, which is glory and light.

How great it would be for the liturgical altar of the divine sacrifice to become for us the mountain of transfiguration that encourages and nourishes us on our journey! This desire is beautifully expressed in a prayer said by the priest at the end of the celebration of the Maronite Liturgy as he kisses the altar:

> Remain in peace, O holy altar of God,
> I hope to return to you in peace.
> May the offering I have received from you forgive
>   my sins
> and prepare me to stand blameless
>   before the throne of Christ.
> I know not whether I will be able to return to you
>   again to offer sacrifice.
> Guard me, O Lord, and protect your holy Church,
> that she may be the way to salvation and the light of
>   the world. Amen.

Called to ascend and called to return to the world, we find strength at the altar for our double mission. There the past and present meet as we recreate and relive past events while remaining in our own day and time. From this vantage point, let me summarize the catechetical principles of the transfiguration, which I will develop further on (see next page).

CATECHETICAL PRINCIPLES OF THE TRANSFIGURATION

1. The disciples are *called* by Jesus to *ascend*:
 a. The disciples are *called to a high mountain*.
 b. The disciples are *called to pray*.
 c. The disciples are *called to be part of God's plan*.

2. The disciples are *called to be sent back down*:
 a. The disciples are *sent to become his living image*.
 b. The disciples are *sent to become his living antennae*.
 c. The disciples are *sent to become a consuming flame*.
 d.The disciples are *sent on a journey*.

Two

In Search of a Living Catechism

Let me pose a question that might at first seem shocking: Do we really need a catechism? I am tempted to say no. Let me explain. To do so, I need to first mention that I am a member of an Eastern Catholic Church, the Maronite Church. This is my point of departure.

The Maronite Living Catechism

In ancient times and well into the modern era, the Syriac Maronite Tradition had no separate book called a "catechism" like the one we know now, no summary of doctrine and morality. Such a book was not needed for our liturgical books used in the Syriac Maronite Tradition were rich in theology, spirituality, and morality—beautiful lessons that the faithful absorbed easily as they came to church on Sunday and other feasts. Embedded in our liturgical books and prayers, these lessons addressed the same three main questions as the *Catechism of the Catholic Church*:

1. Who is God?

2. Who am I?

3. What ought I to be?

By now, perhaps you can see more clearly where I am headed. But bear with me. If you haven't yet put the book down, there is hope that my proposition is not so heretical as it might first appear.

My second consideration—which is even more to the point—is that traditional Maronite life over the centuries has been a living catechism in everyday activities. Three sets of teachers interacted and supported each other: family, church, and community. The family served as the principal teacher. The church served as the second, confirming and strengthening what the family taught. The entire community served as the third, encouraging by example and supervising, sometimes even to the point of directly reprimanding and reporting misdeeds to the family or priest.

With this understanding of Maronite communal assimilation and teaching of catechetical truths, let me again pose the question: Do we really need a catechism? If I wish to be true to my ancient tradition, even though I am a priest, my answer would be "no." To the dismay of many people—even of some from the same Eastern Tradition as myself—who claim that we always had a formal, systematized catechism, I have to counter that we never had one because it was never needed since we lived liturgically in mutually supportive communities. But now the catechism becomes a must for Easterners and Westerners alike.

To understand how this Syriac Maronite Tradition developed, we have to return to the beginnings. This tradition is a branch of the church in which the cross has always been viewed mystically from the twin perspectives of sorrow and glory. We have considered these perspectives intertwined from our earliest days as a community in Antioch. It was here that the followers of Christ were called "Christians" for the first time (Acts 11:26), receiving their faith directly from

Peter and the other apostles. Many were attracted to a priest and hermit named Maron, who died around 410 and was later proclaimed a saint, to share in his life of deep prayer and gift of healing.

In the wake of theological disputes in Antioch regarding the number of natures in Christ, Maron moved away from Antioch with his monks to the banks of the Orontes River. Here they could escape the temptations of the secular Hellenistic world threatening their faith, a quest well imaged in their conversion of a pagan temple into a monastery. The name of this river, the Orontes, is itself an image, almost a metaphor, of the Syriac Maronite Tradition, for in Arabic it is *al'asi*, "the resistant." Indeed this river is resistant, its waters going in the opposite direction from what is expected. So too did Maron and his disciples struggle in their embrace of the mysterious cross, holding fast against the currents of the world, defending God's message, guided by the cross, accepting sufferings, and looking forward to the kingdom of heaven as their true country.

St. Maron's group of monks and hermits constituted a unique spiritual family with a distinct spirituality, belief, and culture. After his death, his spiritual heirs built a monastery dedicated to his memory. Later, still other monasteries were built which became centers of defense for the Christian faith. Around these strongholds the faithful gathered. The community grew under the eventual leadership of its patriarchs and bishops. For some three hundred years, this spiritual family developed and matured, first into a church and then into a whole nation. It was a uniquely independent body centered on its patriarchs.

Maronite spiritual, social, and humanitarian institutions stretched from northern Syria to Lebanon and Palestine. Many thousands were converted from paganism to Christianity by the spiritual heirs of St. Maron, whose name was adopted by his disciples to designate this branch of the Roman Catholic Church.

The peace found by the Maronites in their life near the Orontes would not be a lasting one. At the end of the seventh century, new religious troubles arose—this time terrible persecution—forcing them to move once again. They left their homes and fertile lands in northern Syria and took refuge in the mountains of Lebanon, bringing their most prized possession, the Christian faith, and planting it in their new home.

Thanks to their heroic effort, Lebanon became a Christian land with borders open to all to live and worship in religious and social freedom, which in turn became the backbone of Lebanese independence. From their second home in Lebanon, the Maronites continued to spread their faith and their life style to Rhodes, Cyprus, Palestine, Egypt, Iraq, and the West. The Maronite mystical tradition also continued through the ages, although known by few Western Christians. To this day, the Maronite Church is the only Eastern Church with no corresponding Orthodox branch, a tribute to its robust orthodoxy as well as orthopraxy—putting faith into action in everyday life.

Most important to my questioning the need for a formal catechism is the way the Maronite faith became a living catechism. It made us a "liturgical people" of deep spiritual faith and prayer, able to carry out a life reflecting its solid theology and morality, and in the process producing so many theologians, hermits, and martyrs.

In every prayer and hymn of the Maronite liturgy, biblical theology finds expression. From the beauty and warmth of that expression rather than from duty, the Maronite faithful have memorized those prayers and hymns without effort, often singing or humming them throughout the day at work or home. In this way, the Maronite Church became the gathering (*kanes*) of those "sealed" by the Holy Cross, Father, Son, and Holy Spirit, constantly meeting to glorify the triune God with one heart and one mind.

This trinitarian life was reflected in the three mutually supportive parental, priestly, and communal roles. This threefold strength is again why I can say that we had no need for a catechism, or for what we would call today "specialized catechists," developed as a response to a less integrated time and generation.

You may find it difficult to imagine such a spirit-filled community in which the parents as primary educators were helped in their catechetical task by an entire liturgical people, helped in turn by the priest and the deacon at liturgical gatherings with their offering and explanation of prayers. These gatherings were almost a compendium of theology, spirituality, and morality, wherein children so easily learned their faith that when they became parents themselves they very naturally became the teachers of their own youngsters.

If you do find it difficult to imagine, it is a sign of how far away from a more natural spirituality we have come. But here is the reason I could even dare raise the question of the need for a catechism like the *Catechism of the Catholic Church*. What may seem a negative response to the church's great effort in the publication of this catechism is not at all negative. The catechism is more needed than ever.

The Transfiguration: Exemplar of Catechesis in Daily Life

Even beyond the Maronite example of catechesis in everyday life we find a better one still when we go back to the way Christ himself taught his followers. He did not give his disciples and listeners a theological treatise. No, he first gave them what affected them most, a prayer life, his own "liturgical life" filled with eternal truths. We can see the result: the disciples asked Jesus to teach them how to pray. For all who knew him, event after event of his life provided a living catechism.

To me, the transfiguration—simple but complex as it is—gives us one of the most beautiful liturgical events from Christ's life that can help us understand the threefold mystery of (1) who God is, (2) who we are, and (3) what we ought to be. In every Roman and Maronite celebration of the liturgy, the eucharistic prayer (called "anaphora" in the Maronite Tradition) expresses this theme well:

In Jesus, divinity and humanity are joined

Roman Rite	Maronite Rite
He was conceived through the power of the Holy Spirit, and born of the Virgin Mary, a man like us in all things but sin.... In fulfillment of your will he gave himself up to death; but by rising from the dead, he destroyed death and restored life. And that we might live no longer for ourselves but for him, he sent the Holy Spirit from you, Father... (Eucharistic Prayer IV).	You have united, O Lord, your divinity with our humanity and our humanity with your divinity; your life with our mortality and our mortality with your life. You have assumed what is ours, and you have given us what is yours for the life and salvation of our souls. To you be glory for ever (Anaphora of the Syriac Maronite Church).

You and I know that the living catechism of our ancient ways is almost non-existent in our days. In the big cities, the liturgical community is barely in existence, barely alive, and the secular is overtaking the spiritual. It would not seem that a catechetical community is ever again possible, but through prayer all things are possible. On prayer the threefold Maronite liturgical community was founded. Prayer can not only provide the spark to begin a community but also light its flame anew.

How to do this? The new *Catechism of the Catholic Church* contains a section on exactly this subject. It appears last of all, not to diminish its importance but to complete the other sections.

Prayer and Glory: From Last to First

That is why I propose that in approaching the *Catechism*, we should start at the end with the last chapter first, then return to the beginning. In this way we may understand prayer as our spiritual forebears understood the linkage of the sorrowful and the glorious cross, the far-from-glorious present time, to the time of transfiguration. This is the alpha and the omega of Christian life, as it was the alpha and omega of Christ's life. This fuller understanding comes only through prayer.

Reading the last section on prayer first helps us immerse ourselves in the life of the church, that mysterious river of God's love, presence, and plan of salvation, whereby his living water can be supported and kept from sinking. Having had this foretaste of the glorious life out on the horizon, we can set out from the beginning with our eyes on the cross as sailors look to the mast on which the sail is spread to the winds. In this way, we will surely arrive at the "harbor of salvation," eternal life. The Roman and Maronite liturgies of the Season of the Cross help us take on this perspective:

The cross sets us free

Roman Rite	Maronite Rite
We should glory in the cross of our Lord Jesus Christ, for he is our salvation, our life and our resurrection; through him we are saved and made free (Entrance Song, Feast of the Triumph of the Cross).	Simon Peter guides the boat which is the Church, and the cross is its mast (Fetgomo, Sixth Sunday after Holy Cross).

Transfiguration As Unification

The transfiguration event of the New Testament reflects a similar event in the Old, when Moses received the Ten Commandments on yet another mountain, Mount Sinai. There the faith of Abraham became closely associated with the Law of Moses, which was to be followed even in the desert. This law would become linked with the paschal mysteries of the New Testament as well, for the Ten Commandments cannot be viewed outside the Pasch, which is the cross of Jesus. On the cross, the three elements of faith, law, and liturgy (the paschal celebration) are united. If we separate these elements, we are left with a mere list of rules and prescriptions. But they are one.

We see this unity clearly in retrospect through the cross in the transfiguration, where Jesus, the new Moses and the Paschal Lamb, invites us to the life of the Spirit. The essence of our liturgy is the very place where we Christians fulfill the law to become free and allow the Spirit to transfigure us. The paschal mystery is, then, to be fulfilled in our daily life as we believe in the life, death, and resurrection of Jesus the Christ. Because we are not to keep this understanding and the living of this life to ourselves but share it, loving others as he loved us, this sequence becomes the missionary aspect of our life. Evangelization, catechesis, and religious education become calls to transfiguration and divinization.

The Eucharist becomes not only the source and renewal of moral life but also the pledge of eternal life. In the liturgy, we are invited to follow in the footsteps of him who showed us how to overcome evil. Through Jesus in transfiguration, we too will see ourselves connected to the Old Testament prophets appearing with him on Mount Tabor, Moses and Elijah, who in their lifetime tried so valiantly to penetrate the inner mystery of God (Ex 3 and 1 Kgs 19). Like the disciples on Mount Tabor, we too will see that the vocation of these patriarchs came to its fulfillment in Jesus because he is at the same time fully God and fully man.

Christ's transfiguration gives us an idea of what to expect of our own transfiguration or divinization. He is, in Luke's portrayal, the fulfillment of the prophecy assuring Moses of a successor (Dt 18:15). Jesus is the new Moses, the new Law-giver who will lead us through the exodus from the earthly Jerusalem to the "heavenly Jerusalem" (a term often used in the Syriac Maronite liturgy to express the heavenly kingdom). As the new Moses, Jesus seals the New Covenant with his own blood.

Transfiguration and Liturgy

The connection between the transfiguration event and the liturgy is nothing new to either the Roman or the Syriac Maronite Church. It is clearly expressed in prayers of the Roman Rite Liturgy of the Hours and the Maronite prayers of the Liturgy of the Word and anaphora (eucharistic prayers). Let us see some examples:

We praise God for the Light of transfiguration

Roman Rite	**Maronite Rite**
May he make us an everlasting gift to you and enable us to share in the inheritance of your saints, with Mary, the virgin Mother of God, with the apostles, the martyrs, (Saint N.) and all your saints, on whose constant intercession we rely for help (Eucharistic Prayer III).	Make us worthy to receive these gifts [Body and Blood of Christ], that they may be mingled in our souls and bodies. May they prepare us for the blessed joy of everlasting life which eye has not seen, nor ear heard, nor which has occurred to the heart of man. Therefore, with your saints, we will glorify you, your only-begotten Son and your Holy Spirit, now and forever (Anaphora of St. Celestine).

Roman Rite

You have appeared in glory before the Lord, alleluia, alleluia.

The Lord has clothed you in splendor, alleluia, alleluia.

Glory to the Father, the Son and Holy Spirit. You have appeared in glory before the Lord, alleluia, alleluia (Liturgy of the Hours, Responsory, Evening Prayer I, Transfiguration)

Christ Jesus, you are the splendor of the Father and the perfect image of his being; you sustain all creation with your powerful word and cleanse us of all our sins. On this day you were exalted in glory upon the high mountain (Liturgy of the Hours, Antiphon, Canticle of Mary, Evening Prayer I, Transfiguration).

Lord, in your light may we see light (Liturgy of the Hours, Intercessions, Evening Prayers I and II, Transfiguration).

Maronite Rite

Praise, glory and honor to the Father, who has sent us his only Son, the splendor of his divinity, and one in being with him; to the Son, the eternal splendor of the Father, who humbled himself to come among us in these last days, and revealed the Holy Spirit, who has spoken through the prophets and apostles, the Spirit of truth, who makes us say, "Abba"— Father. To the Good One is due glory and honor this evening, and all the days of our lives, now and for ever. Amen.

O Christ our God, nothing hidden escapes your divine glance. You took on our human nature and became like us in all things but sin, without diminishing yourself or putting aside the perfection of your divinity. Today you desired to give us a picture of your heavenly kingdom, and you appeared in

Roman Rite

Maronite Rite

glory before Peter, James and John, to give them a flavor of the happiness to which you invite us. On this evening, O Lord, we ask you to shine your heavenly light on our spirits and consciences, that we may be enlightened by you, and may contemplate the grandeur of your mercy towards us. As you granted the disciples, so now allow us to taste the sweetness of true happiness, so that with them we may say: "Master, it is good to be here with you. How good it would be to build you a tent among us, so that you could remain with us." How good it is, not only to stay in your house, but that we ourselves become your property and live in and for you.

Lord, how good it is for us to be here; if you wish, let us build three tents here, one for you, one for Moses, and one for Elijah (Liturgy of the Hours, Antiphon 3, Evening Prayer I, Transfiguration).

O God, according to your plan, you have called us to holiness by your grace which you have revealed in Jesus Christ, through your Gospel show to all mankind the glorious splendor of unending life (Liturgy of the Hours, Prayer, Evening Prayer I, Transfiguration).

May this spiritual feast, on which the Church rejoices, increase our joy and happiness. May it confirm those baptized in the faith in your divinity and in confidence in your mercy. May our whole life be built on the hope of encountering you and expectation of the happiness prepared for the elect. Place within us, O Lord, a true love for all, so that without fear or duplicity we may truly witness to this love. May we carry your name among people of every race and

Roman Rite	**Maronite Rite**
	pursue your mission at all times and in all places.
O Christ, you took Peter, James and John and led them up a high mountain by themselves; we pray for our pope and bishops, that they may inspire in your people the hope of being transfigured at the last day (Liturgy of the Hours, Intercessions, Evening Prayer I, Transfiguration).	On this day, O Lord, remember our fathers, the successors of Peter, James, and John, so that they may make your flock feed on wisdom and justice and show it the marvelous beauty of your divinity. Accept our prayers for the whole world, for all the children of the Church, living and dead. Grant us to praise you one day with your saints in happiness and to contemplate the revelation of your face, for ever. Amen.
O Christ, you will reform our lowly body and make it like your glorious one, we pray for our brothers and sisters who have died that they may share in your glory forever (Liturgy of the Hours, Intercessions, Evening Prayer I, Transfiguration).	O Savior, we adore you who offered yourself as a holocaust and pleasing sacrifice. We ask you on the memorial of your transfiguration on the mountain, to accept our prayers and pardon us all sinners. Remember the dead who rest in your hope, and we shall glorify you, now and for ever. Amen (Prayer of Forgiveness and Prayer of Incense, Ramsho, Evening Prayer).

Roman Rite

O Christ, before your passion and death you revealed the resurrection to your disciples on Mount Tabor; we pray for your Church which labors amid the cares and anxieties of this world, that in its trials it may always be transfigured by the joy of your victory (Liturgy of the Hours, Intercessions, Evening Prayer I, Transfiguration).

As we listen to the voice of your Son, help us to become heirs to eternal life with him who lives and reigns with you and the Holy Spirit, one God for ever and ever (Liturgy of the Hours, Prayer, Evening Prayer I, Transfiguration).

Maronite Rite

Praise, glory and honor to the Light, the eternal One from whom proceeds the eternal Light; to the beloved Son, who transfigured himself today on the top of the mountain and has strengthened the faith of his disciples in him; to the Spirit, bearer of life, who is adored with the Father and the Son. To the Good One is due glory and honor this morning, and all the days of our lives, now and for ever. Amen.

O Lord, we thank you for your love and raise our eyes to you, saying: "Show us, O Lord, your mercy, and grant us your salvation." Grant that one day we may hear your voice and partake of the happiness of your paradise. May this feast be a manifestation of your splendor on the Church and the world, and may all see your way and be touched by your light. May your light reach out to all flesh, for your mercy is without limit. We shall glorify you, now and for ever. Amen.

Roman Rite	Maronite Rite
O Christ, you gave light to the world when the glory of the Creator arose over you, we pray for men of good will that they may walk in your light (Liturgy of the Hours, Intercessions, Evening Prayer I, Transfiguration).	O Lord, strengthen us by your will, that we may accomplish the good works of the kingdom of God. May we always contemplate your divine mysteries and be dwelling places for your divinity, now and for ever. Amen (Prayer of Forgiveness and Prayer of Incense, Safro, Morning Prayer).

Crossover through the Liturgy

Since we are "liturgical people," I will rely on the liturgical year and texts of both the Roman and the Syriac Maronite Rites to go through the salvation history expressed in the *Catechism of the Catholic Church*. If we are liturgical people, we will speak a mainly liturgical language and travel a mainly liturgical journey, following from the first coming (Christmas) to the second (the Glorious Cross). The liturgical year and celebrations enable me to do what Christ did at the transfiguration: to provide a foretaste of the second coming to those who would spread his word through the cross of the present to the cross of glory.

As we follow our annual liturgical journey around Christ, his first coming and the later events of his life and ministry will make more sense. They will enable us catechists to get a better grasp of the intimate relationship between the two events so that we can work more effectively with the new catechism and, through it, help our students in the faith.

Summary

What I have been discussing in this chapter is the opening of a window to the followers of Christ to help them see the glorious cross that transforms the present cross of sorrow. This has been the focus of catechesis since it began in the church and is thus the reason why understanding historical catechetical development is necessary before studying the new *Catechism of the Catholic Church*.

Three

Toward a Liturgical Perspective: Catechesis in History

God's call to all Christians is to become "liturgical people"—"sons and daughters of the resurrection," in the words of the Syriac Maronite Liturgy. This call is the same to those in the Western Church as to those in the Eastern. It is particularly important for catechists but it also applies to all people of faith. To be liturgical people means to live with Christ the events of his life with Easter as their source through the liturgical year.

The importance of the Sunday liturgy and the seasons of the liturgical year transfigure the year, as the new *Catechism of the Catholic Church* expresses it:

> 1167 Sunday is the pre-eminent day for the liturgical assembly, when the faithful gather "to listen to the word of God and take part in the Eucharist, thus calling to mind the Passion, Resurrection, and glory of the Lord Jesus, and giving thanks to God who 'has begotten them again, by the resurrection of Jesus Christ from the dead' unto a living hope":

> When we ponder, O Christ, the marvels
> fulfilled on this day,....we say: "Blessed is
> Sunday, for on it began creation...the world's
> salvation...the renewal of human race....On
> Sunday heaven and earth rejoiced and the
> whole universe was filled with light....on it
> were opened the gates of paradise....
> [Fanqîth, *The Syriac Office of Antioch*, vol. 6,
> first part of Summer, 193 B].

The *Catechism* continues:

> 1168 Beginning with the Easter Triduum as its
> source of light, the new age of the resurrection fills
> the whole liturgical year with its brilliance.
> Gradually, on either side of this source, the year is
> transfigured by the liturgy. It really is a "year of
> the Lord's favor." The economy of salvation is at
> work within the framework of time, but since its
> fulfillment in the Passover of Jesus and the
> outpouring of the Holy Spirit, the culmination of
> history is anticipated "as a foretaste," and the
> kingdom of God enters into our time.

> 1169 Therefore *Easter* is not simply one feast
> among others, but the "Feast of feasts," the
> "Solemnity of solemnities," just as the Eucharist is
> the "Sacrament of sacraments" (the Great
> Sacrament)....

> 1171 In the liturgical year the various aspects of
> the one Paschal mystery unfold. This is also the
> case with the cycle of feasts surrounding the
> mystery of the incarnation (Annunciation,
> Christmas, Epiphany)....

The new *Catechism*'s focus on the liturgical year as flowing from the light of Easter underlies my own proposition that catechists begin the new catechetical year by viewing the transfiguration as the window to help Christ's disciples see beyond to the glorious cross transformed by the resurrection. But this focus is exactly how catechesis and religious education began in the church. That is why a short history of catechesis would be in order at this point.

The Meaning of Catechesis

In the early church, "catechesis" signified both the instruction given those preparing for baptism or the books used for that purpose. Today, the word is applied to any instruction aimed at deepening Christian faith, even if addressed to those who are already baptized (CIC 773-80). No matter how the word is used, catechesis in the early Church was the responsibility of the whole community rather than just official teachers, and this community dimension is encouraged by the church today.

The Didache

To begin the study of catechetical history, we need to go back to the apostolic fathers. The oldest catechetical work of that period is the anonymous *Didache* (Gr. "teaching"). Dating from the first century, it was compiled from various sources by a Jewish-Christian author from western Syria or eastern Asia Minor. Some modern scholars wish to exclude these fathers on the basis of their probably not being directly connected with the apostles and that they differed somewhat from New Testament mentality. But their writings shed important light on the development of catechesis from the New Testament church to post-apostolic Christianity.

The *Didache*, or Doctrine of the Apostles, bases its directives on the evangelical tradition of the Sermon on the Mount. The entire document has sixteen chapters: chapters one through ten relate to catechesis, morality, and liturgy; chapters eleven through fifteen include disciplinary regulation; and chapter sixteen deals with the Parousia.

In the liturgical section (chapters one through six), we find descriptions of how to instruct catechumens about their two choices: the Way of Life and the Way of Death. The Way of Life is centered on love of God and love of neighbor as oneself, avoiding evil, and pursuing good. Contrasted with this blessed way is the cursed Way of Death. The *Didache* gives many specifics about both virtues and vices.

Chapters seven through ten are more important to the history of the mystery of liturgy, describing baptism, fasting and prayer, and the Eucharist. We learn that baptism was by immersion in running water and—in emergencies—by infusion. This is the only reference we have from the first two centuries concerning baptism by infusion, which shows that the baptismal formula does not come from theology but from an evangelical tradition.

The *Didache* instructs that the minister and candidate for baptism are to fast. Fasting is also recommended on special days: not "like the hypocrites" on Monday and Thursday but on the fourth day and the Day of Preparation, Wednesday and Friday. Instruction on prayer is joined to teaching on fasting. The Our Father quoted in the *Didache* is almost the same as the text of Matthew (6:9-13), and if we consider the final doxology, we see that the Our Father is a liturgical text.

The eucharistic prayers presented in the *Didache* are very ancient as well as beautiful. The literary genre is that of the Jewish *berakah* ("blessing," "Eucharist"). In describing Jesus as the "servant" like David, we get the impression that the Christian community defined its Christology by its relation with David. The *Didache* closely connects the Eucharist to baptism, specifying that only baptized people could receive the Eucharist, for the Lord had commanded "not to give to dogs what is sacred."

The eucharistic blessing is not presented as grace or as a consecration or a communion in the ordinary sense. Rather, it is viewed as one of the works of God that can evoke only joy and admiration. The image is developed of bread broken and scattered over the mountains, which then becomes one bread, with the prayer that the church may be gathered from the ends of the earth.

The eucharistic breaking of the bread is clarified in the *Didache*. The bread suggests the concept of life and its wonders, bringing closer the concept of the resurrection of Jesus, who is alive and shares with us both life and knowledge, gathering us into the kingdom. Thus the liturgy becomes a vigil, a hopeful wait for that kingdom which arrives in the perspective of the Lord's resurrection and also in his actual return. Within the church, Jesus' followers are brought to unity (many grains forming one bread) and holiness (one must belong to the church to receive this bread).

The Eucharist is concluded by giving thanks to God and asking him to fully gather his church from the four corners of the earth into the kingdom he has prepared. Confession of sins (most likely a liturgical confession such as the Confiteor in the Roman Rite or the Prayer of Forgiveness in the Syriac Maronite Church) is very important before partaking of the Eucharist because, as the *Didache* points out, the faithful should not come to prayer with a guilty conscience.

Other Early Catechetical Sources

Three other early sources in the apostolic tradition on catechesis and liturgy regarding Christian initiation are Justin's *Apology* (I, 61), Tertullian's treatise *On Baptism*, and in particular Hippolytus' *Apostolic Tradition*. In these early writings, we see that initiation involved a solid formal presentation of instructional material in three steps:

1. A lengthy catechetical preparation of the candidates with very specific requirements; for instance, candidates must have a sponsor and should be ready to change occupation, if necessary.

2. An immediate preparation by fasting, prayer, and solemn promises. The prominence of the community's role is clear; for instance, the sponsor spoke for the candidate, whose evaluation consisted in his way of life.

3. Finally, the solemnity of baptism itself. Along with the baptismal ritual came anointing, the laying on of hands, and admission to the common worship of the faithful, where the new members of the church could finally be included in the kiss of peace and the Eucharist.

Our modern *Rite of Christian Initiation of Adults* is a reawakening of and return to the theology of the ancient church. It is also a challenge for catechists, religious educators, and liturgists to blend the past, present, and future into a meaningful present reality.

Later fathers who influenced catechesis and helped bring it to its heights include Cyril of Jerusalem in the East and Ambrose and Augustine in the West. Among their most important characterizations of early church catechesis are these:

- The community framework in which the Word of God was proclaimed, explained, reflected upon, and lived out.

- The example, prayer, and support of the community.

- The highly important place of the cross.

The Catechetical Reduction

In the fourth and fifth centuries, when baptism in childhood became more common than in adulthood, there was a parallel change in catechesis. Until the end of the fifteenth century, catechesis became reduced to some instruction and to Sunday preaching on the Creed, Commandments, and prayers.

The Rise of Catechisms

In the mid-sixteenth century, catechisms became influential in catechesis. First in print were Protestant versions, which soon inspired Catholic editions.

The Protestant Challenge

Martin Luther's catechism, appearing in 1529, was divided into three parts: the Commandments, the Creed, and the Lord's Prayer and Meal. Luther's purpose in writing this catechism was to form people of action who would live out the truth, not just talk about it. Emphasizing the "Pure Word of God," the Bible, he laid great emphasis on the Commandments in order to build a strong human foundation on which to build an even stronger divine foundation.

Catholic Catechisms

It was not long before Catholics noticed the success of Luther's catechism and made their own attempts, notably Peter Canisius in Germany (1555), the Fathers of the Council of Trent (1566), and Robert Bellarmine in Italy (1597). Trent's catechism was divided into four parts: the Creed, Sacraments, Commandments, and Our Father. Its catechetical aim was knowledge of Christ, love of God, and observance of the Commandments.

Robert Bellarmine's was the most popular of the Catholic catechisms. Using a question-and-answer format and directed at both adults and children, Bellarmine expected memorization of his catechism. His topic order differed from Trent's: it began with the Creed but followed with the Our Father, Commandments, and Sacraments. The catechetical project of the First Vatican Council a few centuries later was based on Bellarmine's catechism.

But catechesis had strayed from the catechesis of the early church. Just one example can serve to show how far.

Bellarmine's considered the sacraments as "tools" or "means of grace." By contrast, in early catechesis, the mysteries and the sacraments they reenacted were understood as participatory events in the saving acts of Christ's passion, death and resurrection. A catechist from the early church would have been bewildered at such a utilitarian approach!

Manual and Method

With the rise of catechisms, catechesis became identified with a printed manual. From the seventeenth century on, the emphasis in religious education was on methods of teaching catechism. Some of the most important methodologies were the "Method of St. Sulpice" popularized by Jean Jacques Olier (1608-1657) and the works of Claude Fleury (1640-1723) and St. Jean Baptiste de la Salle (1651-1715).

The Method of St. Sulpice is of interest for its pedagogical detail. It comprised a ten-stage plan:

PART I

1. Entrance: The children entered in silence, and everyone genuflected. Opening prayer was followed by the singing of hymns.

2. Questioning: The catechist interrogated children from the pulpit, each child arising and making the Sign of the Cross before answering.

3. Competition: The catechist posed prolonged questions of his choice to the students who made the best grades.

4. Recitation of the Gospel: The catechist asked each child to recite certain lines from the Gospel, requiring the next child to take up from where the other left off.

5. Report on homework: This included the work of the student and the help given by parents.

PART II

6. Instruction: The singing of hymns preceded and concluded a thirty-minute instruction.

PART III

7. Announcements: In an attempt to help create and form a communal spirit, the head catechist discussed the students' progress, explained the feast days, mentioned families with sick members, and so forth. Again a hymn was sung. This was an attempt to foster a communal spirit.

8. Homily: First kneeling on the altar steps, the catechist would then mount the pulpit with the Gospels and, after the reading of the Gospel, would offer remarks. Yet another hymn was sung.

9. Point awards.

10. Dismissal in procession.

Some two centuries later, Napoleon authorized an "imperial catechism" (1806) for use in France to maintain instructional uniformity. Such a notion of a catechism to be used throughout a political sphere was discussed by the First Vatican Council (1869-70). Although Vatican I gave approval to the idea of a universal catechism, it was never implemented due to external strife.

The United States' Catechetical Effort

In the United States, of course, a national catechetical effort had begun in 1829 when the Third Plenary Council of

Baltimore authorized the writing of a uniform catechism. The result was the *Baltimore Catechism*, published in 1885.

Famous as it became, however, Baltimore was not the only important catechetical movement in the United States. Another was Dom Virgil Michel's efforts earlier in this century to stress the role of liturgy in catechesis. For Michel, liturgy is "incarnate catechesis," a "living catechesis." The understanding of liturgy, he believed, would help children and adults alike to understand the church, its history, its theology, its spirituality—in other words "its spirit."

Although these insights were brought to the United States from the European liturgical movement, Michel's particular contribution was in presenting religion as something to be lived instead of something merely to be learned. His idea of incorporating social justice into the liturgy would later be echoed in the Catechetical Directory, entitled *Sharing the Light of Faith*.

This brings us up to the present. There is no need to go into detail about modern-day catechesis in the United States for it has been addressed by different documents such as the Catechetical Directory and various documents of the U.S. Catholic bishops. What we find in the catechetics of the past thirty years is emphasis on the need to draw from the social sciences, so the focus is now on issues such as methodology, socialization, and acculturation.

A typical modern lesson outline might be something like the following:

1. Begin with the Sign of the Cross or a short prayer.

2. Express the theme of the lesson.

3. Greet the children.

4. Sing a hymn.

5. Explain the subject material.

6. Sing a hymn related to the topic.

7. Formulate a prayer related to the topic.

8. Prepare students or introduce them to Scripture readings.

9. Do the reading(s).

10. Give a short explanation ending with the renewal of faith.

Catechesis in the Liturgy

I would like to compare these so-called modern methods to the structure of the Syriac Maronite Liturgy of the Word, which is one of the oldest liturgies of the Catholic Church. Our Maronite Rite closely parallels the Method of St. Sulpice but within a solemn liturgical framework. Century after century, the aim of this liturgy has been to form its worshipers into a liturgical people journeying toward the heavenly Jerusalem where the heavenly liturgy is eternally celebrated. Indeed, this liturgical approach was the only way to explain the truth in the early church. Through the Sunday liturgy as well as the Liturgy of the Hours, God's plan of salvation was unfolded and explained.

The Liturgy of the Maronite Rite parallels the Liturgy of the Roman Rite in many ways, but it differs in several aspects of catechetical interest, particularly the Prayer of Forgiveness (Hoosoyo), which presents to the faithful the specific subject matter of the feast being celebrated.

As an example of how the Syriac Maronite Liturgy developed this teaching of God's plan of salvation, I will take an excerpt from the regular Sunday liturgy, for every Sunday is a commemoration of the resurrection, as the *Catechism of the Catholic Church* notes, reflecting the "Great Feast," our term for Easter. Following are the main points of the Syriac Maronite Liturgy of the Word:

1. Doxology (Sign of the Cross)

2. Opening prayer (expressing the purpose of our gathering:

   > O Lord, grant us tranquility and peace through the blessings of the day of your glorious resurrection, that, in company with your heavenly hosts, we may give you glory and thanksgiving, now and for ever.

3. Greeting:

   > Peace be with the Church and her children.

4. Hymn:

   > Glory to God in the highest and peace on earth and good will to all.

5. Prayer of Forgiveness (the Hoosoyo)

   > May we offer glory, praise, and honor to the good and merciful Lord: willing to become flesh and taste death, he descended to the abyss and saved us from death itself. Through his resurrection he filled his disciples with joy and enlightened the nations by the light of his salvation. To you, O Christ, are due glory and honor this Sunday and all the days of our lives, and for ever. Amen.

   > O Word of God, who can praise the depth of your mercy? And what voice is able to bless you, who are above all blessing? Mind and tongue fail to describe the wonders you accomplished on that holy and glorious day, the Sunday of your resurrection from the dead.

   > With the Psalmist David we proclaim: This is the day the Lord has made, let us rejoice and celebrate. This is the day that has no equal in

the past nor in the future. This is the great feast day, crown and glory of all feasts.

And now, O Christ our Lord, we petition you through the fragrance of this incense, which we offer you: pardon our faults; give peace to the troubled and consolation to the sorrowful; bring back those who are far away and watch over those who are near; guide our shepherds, protect your priests, and sanctify the deacons; forgive sinners, guard the just, sustain orphans, and support those who are widowed; prevent dissension and put an end to conflicts; remember the faithful departed and grant them rest in your heavenly kingdom, so that in their company we may celebrate the feast that has no end, and glorify you, your blessed Father, and your living Holy Spirit, for ever. Amen.

6. Hymn (proper to the explanation):

At the dawn of the day, like the just Abraham, let us join for prayer and offering. And on that day, which is coming in glory, let us go to meet the living God. Alleluia!

On Sunday, the day of light, let us praise and give thanks to our King and Savior. In his love he came to us, and with his might he liberated Adam and his children. Alleluia!

On the Sunday of the end of time, when, surrounded by hosts of light and spirit, you will come to judge all nations, make us worthy, O Lord, to meet you and sing of your glory in the company of your saints. Alleluia!

7. Prayer (related to the topic):

Be pleased, O Lord, with the sweet fragrance of this incense. Make us worthy to proclaim your rising from the dead with your holy

angels; to announce your resurrection with
your women disciples; and to rejoice in your
triumph with your blessed apostles. We
glorify you, O Christ, your Father, and your
Holy Spirit, for ever. Amen.

8. Preparation or introduction to the
   Scripture readings—Prayer and Psalm of
   the readings:

   Trisagion:

   Holy are you, O God;
   Holy are you, O Strong One;
   Holy are you, O Immortal One,
   have mercy on us (three times).

   O holy and immortal Lord,
   sanctify our minds and purify our
   consciences, that we may praise you with pure
   hearts
   and listen to your Holy Scriptures.
   To you be glory, for ever.

   Come in peace, O Sunday,
   that great and blessed day.
   God's angels and mortals find joy in you
   and celebrate.

   Let us proclaim that great and blessed day
   from mountain tops,
   and let angels and mortals sing praise
   to the Lord.

   Blessed is the Lord who exalted Sunday
   above all other days,
   with hymns, praise, and priests
   to proclaim the good news.

9. Readings:

   After the first reading:

   Alleluia! Alleluia! This is the day the Lord has
   made. Let us rejoice and celebrate! Alleluia!

After the reading of the Gospel that ends
with "This is the truth. Peace be with you,"
the people respond:

Praise and blessings to Jesus Christ for his
living word to us.

10. Homily and Creed (explanation and
    expression of faith in the lesson)

Summary

Catechesis in the early church took place in the midst of
community life during the stages of the pre-catechumenate
(a time of evangelization); the catechumenate (the Rite of
Election); enlightenment and reception of the sacraments or
mysteries of initiation (baptism, confirmation/chrismation,
and Eucharist); and mystagogia (post-baptismal catechesis
during Easter week).

This same sequence is a good one for us today, continuing
to work through the ancient liturgical texts to help us make
the journey to Emmaus with Jesus, the Pastor, who will
encounter us and lead us to catechesis, then to the liturgy,
then to mystagogia and zeal for mission, the telling of our
story to the "stranger" who joins us on our journey. To do
this, we must listen to him as he retells the story in biblical
terms and background so that we may recognize who he
really is, who we are, and what we ought to be. This will
require a new vision, one that overlays the sorrowful and the
glorious cross into a unity.

Four

In Search of a Vision and a Foretaste

One of the sayings in the Book of Proverbs shows our human need for an idea of where we're going: "Without prophecy the people become demoralized"—or alternately translated, "the people perish" (Prv 29:18). But what is "vision"? Dictionaries tell us there are several meanings. Beyond the faculty or sense of sight, vision is defined at least four other ways:

- the ability to anticipate

- insight; imagination

- a mental representation or manifestation of, or as of, external objects, or scenes, as in religious revelation or dreams

- something seen; especially, something or someone very beautiful or pleasing

These four definitions have one common thread: they involve seeing something unique, different, or mysterious. It is in this vein that the *Catechism of the Catholic Church* sees the transfiguration of Jesus: as a vision that gives a foretaste of the kingdom:

554 From the day Peter confessed that Jesus is the Christ, the Son of the living God, the Master "began to show his disciples that he must go to Jerusalem and suffer many things...and be killed, and on the third day be raised."....

555 For a moment Jesus discloses his divine glory, confirming Peter's confession. He also reveals that he will have to go by the way of the cross at Jerusalem in order to "enter into his glory." Moses and Elijah had seen God's glory on the Mountain; the Law and the Prophets had announced the Messiah's sufferings....

556 On the threshold of the public life: the baptism; on the threshold of the Passover: the Transfiguration. Jesus' baptism proclaimed "the mystery of the first regeneration," namely, our Baptism; the Transfiguration "is the sacrament of the second regeneration": our own Resurrection....The Transfiguration gives us a foretaste of Christ's glorious coming, when he "will change our lowly body to be like his glorious body."...

I would like to expand here on this particular passage of St. Luke's Gospel that describes the transfiguration of Jesus Christ:

About eight days after he said this, he took Peter, John, and James and went up the mountain to pray. While he was praying his face changed in appearance and his clothing became dazzling white. And behold, two men were conversing with him, Moses and Elijah, who appeared in glory and spoke of his exodus that he was going to accomplish in Jerusalem. Peter and his companions had been overcome by sleep, but becoming fully awake, they saw his glory and the two men standing with him. As they were about to part from him, Peter said to Jesus, "Master, it is good that we are here; let us make three tents, one

for you, one for Moses, and one for Elijah." But he
did not know what he was saying. While he was still
speaking, a cloud came and cast a shadow over
them, and they became frightened when they
entered the cloud. Then from the cloud came a
voice that said, "This is my chosen Son; listen to
him." After the voice had spoken, Jesus was found
alone. They fell silent and did not at that time tell
anyone what they had seen (Lk 9:28-36).

What an unusual, intriguing "vision." At first reading, this
passage seems to be at one and the same time easy to grasp
but difficult to explain, simple but complicated, under-
standable but mysterious. Whereas light normally helps us
see things clearly, as we read this particular passage, the light,
though dazzling, also raises many questions. Why were Moses
and Elijah present? Why did the apostles fall asleep? Why did
the cloud envelop Jesus and the prophets?

Transfiguration As Radical Change

How do we explain this passage? There are many ways.
A good place to begin is to continue with some of the
meanings of key words in the passage, beginning with the
word "transfiguration" itself. Its origin is from the Latin
transfigurare from *trans*, "beyond," and *figura*, "figure." The
word connotes radical change, complete transformation in
figure or appearance, often glorious, as in the sudden ema-
nation of radiance from Jesus on the mountain.

The setting of the transfiguration has a number of interesting points to keep in mind. Jesus was on a mountain.
Mountains were often the place where God historically chose
to manifest himself or reveal a message. Jesus was in prayer,
in the presence of the One who sent him, the One who brings
out his best: his Father. Jesus was also with his special friends,
Peter, who would become head of the church; James, who
would be his first witness; and John, the one Jesus particularly
loved. Jesus was intimately united with his Father, who pub-

licly announced him as his Son who was to suffer and die but also alluded to his glory to come.

Jesus spoke with Moses and Elijah, witnesses of the past who confirmed that Jesus is the one they spoke of, the one who would suffer, die, and be resurrected. Paralleling the role of these prophets is the role of the apostles, for they too were witnesses of Christ, although at the time alive and observers of the event. The transfiguration would help their faith confront the passion they would undergo as well as anticipate the resurrection that would be theirs.

Prayer As Key

A simple, practical approach to the transfiguration that can help irrespective of culture, age, or understanding is to place ourselves alongside the apostles on Mount Tabor. We too are weary from the ascent of the mountain and full of questions raised by the events. No doubt the apostles had difficulty finding answers. Jesus must have tried to answer some of their questions, but how much did that help?

In the midst of all the confusion and unanswered questions, one thing in particular must have helped the apostles: the attitude of Jesus in prayer. Later, after the resurrection, they could understand better how the sorrowful and glorious crosses of the past and future can be joined, how it is possible even in time of present trouble, even suffering and death, to look over the horizon to glory. To arrive at this glorious future, they had to accept the cross of the present.

This difficult point is well expressed in Maronite liturgical passages from an entire season devoted to the Holy Cross. We celebrate on September 14—as does the Roman Rite—a feast which we call the Feast of the Exaltation of the Holy, Life-giving Cross and which the Romans call the Feast of the Triumph of the Cross, but we also celebrate an entire season for seven Sundays thereafter. The Roman Rite has no corresponding season. Each of the Maronite Sundays of this season presents exquisite imagery to lift hearts to the lifted Christ, such as the following:

We praise God for the cross of Christ

Roman Rite	Maronite Rite
Eternal Son of the Father, you came to cast fire on the earth and you longed to see its flame kindled in the hearts of all men, grant that through holiness of life we may come to share in the undying light of your glory (Liturgy of the Hours, Intercessions, Morning Prayer, Triumph of the Cross).	The cross is a lighthouse scattering the darkness death brings. For the face of the Savior lights the way and leads us on to his place of joy (Mazmooro, Sunday of the Faithful Departed).
We adore you, O Christ, and we praise you, because by your cross you have redeemed the world (Gospel Verse, Triumph of the Cross).	The cross of Christ secures the foundations of the earth. Blessed is the holy gospel that flows from it (Korozooto, Exaltation of the Holy, Life-giving Cross).
How radiant is that precious cross which brought us our salvation. In the cross we are victorious, through the cross we shall reign, by the cross all evil is destroyed, alleluia (Liturgy of the Hours, Morning Prayer, Triumph of the Cross).	The pillar of fire and Jacob's ladder disappeared. But the cross is forever and lights the sky for the children of man to ascend to the Father (Fetgomo, Fourth Week after the Exaltation of the Holy, Life-giving Cross).
	The wisdom of the cross is foolishness to unbelievers, but life to those who know the Lord's voice (Korozooto, Seventh Sunday after the Holy Cross).

Like these beautiful images that show us a cross transfigured into the service of light and strength, we find in Jesus' prayer on Mount Tabor a prayer of vision into the coming of the spiritual kingdom. Again and again we climb Mount Tabor; again and again we see Jesus confronted by the double measure of sorrow and the glory to come. It should exhaust us. So too should working our way through the *Catechism of the Catholic Church*. Through prayer like Christ's and a short rest, our vision can be clearer to rise to still more difficult challenges. Like the apostles on the mountain, we should learn three things from the transfiguration which are in turn the three focuses of the *Catechism*: who God is; who we are; and what we ought to be.

Once again we look to the liturgy to see these same points. They are expressed clearly in the beautiful words of the Roman and Maronite Rites:

The light of Tabor highlights the mystery of Jesus

Roman Rite	Maronite Rite
In the shining cloud the Spirit is seen; from it the voice of the Father is heard: This is my Son, my beloved, in whom is all my delight. Listen to him (Entrance Song, Transfiguration).	May we be worthy to praise, confess and glorify the bright Light of eternal Father Who made known to us the triune mystery of divinity. Today He reveals Himself on Mount Tabor and shows His disciples the glory that was His from the beginning. Let us worship and bless Him, one holy God, Father, Son and Spirit, now and forever. Amen.

Roman Rite

Today the Lord was transfigured and the voice of the Father bore witness to him; Moses and Elijah appeared with him in glory and spoke with him about the death he was to undergo.

The law was given through Moses and prophecy through Elijah. Radiant in the divine majesty, they were seen speaking with the Lord (Liturgy of the Hours, Antiphones 1 and 2, Morning Prayer, Transfiguration).

Maronite Rite

O Christ our God, you chose to raise our mortal nature and make us companions of Your Spirit. In Your humility You came to earth and taught our race the hidden mystery of Your divinity. With Your light, You led Your people from the slavery of Satan and death. You appeared to Moses in a bush that blazed with fiery brilliance, and there Your divinity was cloaked in mountain mist. Then, when You came to complete Your plan for us, You led Peter, James and John to Mount Tabor. You were cloaked in dazzling brilliance as You were transfigured before their eyes. The Father's voice thundered and split the sky, "This is My beloved Son, hear and know that in us there is no division." Moses and Elias then came to speak to You about the last days, judgment and the fulfillment to your plan. But You cautioned the disciples not to reveal the vision until Your passion and death. In this way, Your plan for mankind would be completed.

Roman Rite	Maronite Rite
O God, you have filled your chosen people with the bounty of your house, grant that we may always find the source of our life in the body of Christ (Liturgy of the Hours, Intercessions, Morning Prayer, Transfiguration).	And now we petition You, O Lord; enlighten Your Church with Your great light. Set her foundations firm in the true faith and grant safety to Christians everywhere. Forgive our debts and grant happy memories to our dead. With them we will praise You, now and forever (Hoosoyo, Prayer of Forgiveness, Transfiguration).

At the closing of the Liturgy of the Word (the Breaking of the Word), and the Anaphora (the Breaking of the Bread, or eucharistic prayer) the Maronite faithful renew these same three points every day as we say the anamnesis (memorial): "We commemorate your death, O Lord. We confess your resurrection. We await your coming." These three statements find a parallel among the faithful of the Roman Rite in their various memorial acclamations, such as "Christ has died, Christ is risen, Christ will come again" and "Dying, you destroyed our death; rising, you restored our life; Lord Jesus, come in glory."

As teachers, it is our task in evangelization and catechesis to commemorate, to confess our belief, and to await the Lord's coming following our journey to the mountain. In other words, we need to become a liturgical people who live the present in light of the past and hope in the future. We need to immerse ourselves in the events of the liturgy, trying to celebrate with ever more awareness so that we actually relive those events with Christ. Let it be our aim to move beyond mere commemoration of past events in the same way that all good Jews try to do as they celebrate Passover. On this feast, they believe that they are mystically united with the

Jews of the actual Passover, freed from bondage along with them into transformation as God's chosen people.

The Liturgical Sabbath Perspective

Something of the same perspective permeates the Jewish Sabbath worship. The *Catechism of the Catholic Church* beautifully expresses how the liturgy transforms the entire year through our Sabbath-day celebrations, which in turn revolve around the events of Easter, in passages that were cited at the beginning of chapter three: numbers 1167, 1168, 1169, and 1171.

These words of the *Catechism* are reflected in yet another Maronite liturgical—and at the same time catechetical—passage about our role in the context of Christ's transfiguration seen from the vantage point of his resurrection.

Christ's resurrection completes the transfiguration

Roman Rite	**Maronite Rite**
On your holy mountain he revealed himself in glory in the presence of his disciples. He had already prepared them for his approaching death. He wanted to teach them through the Law and the Prophets that the promised Christ had first to suffer and so come to the glory of his resurrection (Eucharistic Prayer, Second Sunday of Lent).	O Christ our God, in your resurrection, you have revealed your Mystery more completely than on the day of your transfiguration. On Mount Tabor you appeared as God in perfect human nature and as man in whom dwells the fullness of divinity. The power of God that shone within you did not conceal your humanity, nor did your humanity obscure your divinity. Both dwelt together in perfect harmony. Your appearance on Mount Tabor lasted only a

Roman Rite	Maronite Rite
	moment, and your revelation was only for a chosen few. But what you have revealed by your resurrection is perduring, lasts forever and is for all to see. On Mount Tabor, the radiance of the apparition was only momentary. But the glow of your resurrection floods and inundates both soul and body. On Mount Tabor, Peter was so taken by your revelation that he was moved to say: "It is good for us to be here, Lord." And now, O Lord, your Church, strengthened by your passion and encouraged by your resurrection, proclaims for her children: "It is good for us to be here, Lord."
He has made us children of the light, rising to new and everlasting life. He has opened the gates of heaven to receive his faithful people. His death is our ransom from death; his resurrection is our rising to life (Eucharistic Prayer II, Easter).	May we ascend to the heights and rise in your resurrection. With the burning of this incense, may we put off the heavy garments of the past and clothe ourselves with the shining, perfumed garments of light and gladness. Then, as sons and daughters of light, we shall praise and glorify you, your glorious Father and your eternal Spirit, now and forever (Hoosoyo, Prayer of Forgiveness, Fifth Sunday of Resurrection).

Roman Rite	Maronite Rite
	Greater than that of Mount Tabor and more glorious then that of Bethlehem is the revelation of your victory over death. For now you reign eternally, and your triumph is for all to see (Mazmooro, Fifth Sunday of Resurrection).

Again we have liturgical passages which in very simple catechesis tell us who God is, who we are, and what we ought to be. It encourages us in our lifelong journey as liturgical people "clothed with the shining perfumed garments of light and gladness" of transfiguration and resurrection, already living eternity.

Life of Faith: Mirror of the Transfiguration

Considering "evangelization" and "catechesis" in the same way as the liturgical texts above, baptism becomes a reality mirroring the transfiguration. The message is that if we live our faith as sons or daughters of God, with our whole heart and mind and all our strength, three things will result:

1. We will hear the voice of the heavenly Father saying, "This is my beloved son/daughter, who like Jesus is ready to accept the cross as a personal mission. Listen to him/her."

2. Our faces will reflect the light of our unity with our Father, never conveying any other message.

3. The present will become a reality to be
   lived, not escaped. Although we, like the
   apostles, might prefer setting up a tent
   and settling down on the heights, like
   them we are invited to go back down with
   Jesus and serve others as he did, finding
   our real glory in this cross.

What beautiful service is ours in catechetics: to provide
our students with this glimpse of the transfigured Lord so
that they understand better where they are going in light of
his—and thus their own—true identity. Perhaps helping our
students discover their true identity is not something we
consider a main purpose. Yet it is something they always
hunger for, particularly in a culture where so many people
have trouble knowing who they really are and what their
glorious destiny really is. The transfiguration takes on another aspect: the promise of discovery of these very things.

The events of Mount Tabor, in retrospect through the
cross of Easter, far surpass all our lesson plans and materials.
"Where there is no vision, the people will get out of hand."
This vision is the window through which the glory of eternity
is seen. Descending from Mount Tabor, the cross of the
present is both cause and fulfillment of the vision, a foretaste
of the kingdom.

The *Catechism of the Catholic Church* provides a window and
a vision for all members of the church in all their varied
needs:

- For bishops, doctors of the faith, it will
  serve as a resource.

- For priests, it will assist in teaching and
  preaching as well as in ongoing personal
  formation.

- For theologians, it will be a reference for
  doctrinal orthodoxy and fidelity in teaching.

- For catechists, it will provide a preparation tool for teaching the Word.

- For writers and publishers, it will guide them with their catechetical materials.

- For all the faithful, it will help deepen their faith as it clarifies beliefs.

Summary

To all of us, the new catechism should be seen as an "ecclesial event" through which the church speaks a single language and as an "instrument of communion" because it will serve as the main foundation, unifying all catechetical programs. As such and in summary, this catechism should be seen as a "transfiguration event," a window, a foretaste, an encounter with the God who loves us and through the cross of the present will bring out the best in us as he prepares us for eternal life.

Five

Why the Glorious Cross?

With an understanding of the need for vision to draw us onward, we return to the cross as presented in both the new catechism and the liturgy. Raised high in both sources, the torch of the glorious cross shines upon the sorrowful cross to light our way. In the glow of the cross of glory which provides backlighting, the cross of sorrow begins to take on the transcendence of the cross of glory.

But because Jesus Christ is one of the Trinity, so too is his cross linked with the Father and the Holy Spirit. We need to look at this mystery.

Trinitarian Christocentrism in the Catechism

In the Syriac Maronite liturgy, after the preparation for communion, the priest elevates the paten and the chalice, saying: "Holy things for the holy, with perfection, purity and sanctity," and the congregation responds:

> One holy Father; one holy Son; one Holy Spirit.
> Blessed be the name of the Lord, for he is one in
> heaven and on earth, to him be glory for ever.

This summarizes the teaching of the *Catechism of the Catholic Church*, which is trinitarian and Christocentric:

The Trinity is the most important of our beliefs

234 The mystery of the Most Holy Trinity is the
central mystery of Christian faith and life. It is the
mystery of God in himself. It is therefore the
source of all the other mysteries of faith, the light
that enlightens them....

To be truthful and faithful to the "hierarchy of the truths
of faith" would be to clearly emphasize the Trinity. Indeed
the *Catechism of the Catholic Church* was faithful to the trinitarian approach as it treated the topics of creation, church,
liturgy and prayer, and to keeping Christ as the center:

Jesus is our model

520 In all of his life Jesus presents himself as *our
model.* He is "the perfect man," who invites us to
become his disciples and follow him....

This statement recalls our earlier discussion of the transfiguration, the place it gives the cross, and how it includes the
liturgy. The *Catechism* clearly emphasizes the role of the cross
in Christian life:

From the cross, Jesus reigns

550 The coming of God's kingdom means the
defeat of Satan's....Jesus' *exorcisms* free some
individuals from the domination of demons....The
kingdom of God will be definitively established
through Christ's cross: "God reigned from the
wood."

From the cross, Jesus draws us

662 ...The lifting up of Jesus on the cross signifies
and announces his lifting up by his Ascension into
heaven, and indeed begins it. Jesus Christ, the one
priest of the new and eternal Covenant, "entered...
heaven itself, now to appear in the presence of
God on our behalf." There Christ permanently
exercises his priesthood, for he "always lives to
make intercession"....

Trinitarian Christocentrism in the Liturgy

Having summarized the previous chapters in the above passages, I wish to emphasize in this chapter the place and importance of the cross, which becomes our victorious and glorious cross in the Roman and Maronite liturgies. This I will do with the Maronite Prayers of Forgiveness of the Feast of the Exaltation of the Holy, Life-giving Cross, which are an entire catechesis by themselves, joining theology and dogma into a unique form of prayer; and with several prayers from the Mass and the Liturgy of the Hours of the Roman Rite.

We glorify God for our glorious redemption

Roman Rite	Maronite Rite
God our Father, in obedience to you your only Son accepted death on the cross for the salvation of mankind. We acknowledge the mystery of the cross on earth. May we receive the gift of redemption in heaven (Prayer, Morning Prayer, Triumph of the Cross).	Praise, glory and honor to the heavenly Father, who sent his beloved Son for our redemption; to the Savior, who has accomplished our redemption by the power of the gospel, allowing them to plant the standard of the cross in the universe, so that all the nations might bow before him. To the Good One is due glory and honor this evening, and all the days of our lives, now and for ever. Amen.

Roman Rite

We adore you, O Christ, and we bless you, by your holy cross you have redeemed the world (Responsory, Morning Prayer, Triumph of the Cross).

He is the true and eternal priest who established this unending sacrifice.
He offered himself as a victim for our deliverance...
(Preface, Holy Eucharist I, Mass of the Lord's Supper, Holy Thursday).

Maronite Rite

Christ Jesus our Lord and Savior, today we commemorate your cross of life. Through it you have erased the debt of our sins and have rendered all things new. The cross is the foundation of victory and triumph; the hope of believers and the source of life; it is the key of heaven and the wood of salvation; the cross is the light of the universe and the torch of the right path. The cross is the foundation of the Church and the emblem of our victory; it is our power and honor, the strength of the apostles and the language of the preachers; the cross is the assurance of faith, the joy of hope and the perfection of love. We are marked by the cross at baptism and we walk in the way of salvation. By the cross our sacrifice is rendered perfect and our sins are forgiven. By the cross the priestly service is accomplished and by it we are blessed. By the cross our sick are healed and our souls are enlightened.

Roman Rite	**Maronite Rite**
O cross, you are the glorious sign of our victory. Through your power may we share in the triumph of Christ Jesus (Liturgy of the Hours, Canticle of Mary, Evening Prayer II, Triumph of the Cross).	And now as we celebrated in joy the victory of the cross, we cry out: "There is neither happiness nor glory, save in the cross of Christ Jesus our Lord." In it the apostles, martyrs and confessors rejoice; from it they draw strength for their struggles, they bear it on their bodies and show it forth to the world which considers it folly. May it console us in our trials, heal our wounds, and be for us a weapon in the arena. May it help us in our weakness and give us joy in sacrifice. May the blessings of Christ our Savior come upon us and we shall adore him, his Father who sent him, and his Spirit who sanctifies us. We ask him to reveal himself to us each day by his cross, so that we might be able to contemplate him one day carrying his glorious cross of light. We shall go to meet him with joy, entering in the procession of the saints and singing glory, for ever. Amen (Hoosoyo, Prayer of Forgiveness, of Ramsho, Evening Prayer of the Maronite Church).

Roman Rite

O Christ, you emptied yourself, taking the form of a servant and being made like us, grant that your people may follow the example of your humility.

O Christ, you humbled yourself and became obedient unto death, even death on a cross, grant that your servants may imitate your obedience and willing acceptance of trials (Liturgy of the Hours, Intercessions, Evening Prayer II, Triumph of the Cross).

The tree of life flourished in the midst of the holy city of Jerusalem, and its leaves had power to save all the nations, alleluia (Liturgy of the Hours, Antiphon 2, Evening Prayer I, Triumph of the Cross).

Son of God, you healed the people of Israel when they looked upon the bronze serpent, protect us this day from the deadly wound of sin.

Son of Man, just as Moses raised up the serpent in the desert, so you were lifted up on the cross in the sight of all the nations, raise us up to share in the triumph of your cross (Liturgy of the Hours,

Maronite Rite

Praise, glory and honor to him who descended from the heights, died and rose for our salvation. He is the One who left his cross in witness to his death, resurrection and victory over death. To the Savior whose triumph the Church celebrates, the Good One is due glory and honor this morning and all the days of our lives, now and for ever. Amen.

O Christ our God, you give life and bestow benefits, you became human, lived among us and accomplished your saving plan by realizing the sayings of the prophets. For our salvation you were willing to be raised on the cross, and the light of your joyous resurrection illuminated the whole world. In paradise, the tree of life symbolized your cross, and Moses showed the sign of the cross when he stretched out his arms for the salvation of the people. The bronze serpent was the symbol of your cross for the life of whoever looked upon it was saved. Your cross was stamped by the "Taw" written on the foreheads of the elect as spoken of by Ezekiel. It is the cross which

Roman Rite	Maronite Rite
Intercessions, Morning Prayer, Triumph of the Cross).	Isaac indicated by the wood of the sacrifice, and the wood of Noah's ark, the vessel of salvation, was its image.
You decreed that man should be saved through the wood of the cross. The tree of man's defeat became his tree of victory; where life was lost, there life has been restored through Christ our Lord (Preface, Masses of the Holy Cross).	And now, we celebrate this spiritual feast with the whole Church and its children scattered throughout the world, as we proclaim: Blessed are you, O holy wood of the cross, symbol of power and honor; Blessed are you, O cross of Christ, raised in our churches and the head of our processions as a sign of victory.
The Lord hung upon the cross to wash away our sins in his own blood. How splendid is that blessed cross (Liturgy of the Hours, Antiphon 2, Morning Prayer, Triumph of the Cross).	Be for us, night and day, the attentive guardian who will not allow the evil one to conquer us. Be the comforter of those whom this base world has deprived of its vain joys. Accompany those who travel, strengthen the sick, give hope to the broken hearted and joy to the afflicted souls. May your sign be printed in the hearts of believers. May they live through you and carry you with zeal in all countries. May they preach you and be clothed themselves with the blessings by the pure blood shed on you. O Christ, may we who are signed with the sign of the victorious and faithful cross remain faithful to that seal by which we have been marked. May

Roman Rite	Maronite Rite
	we be worthy to see your cross of light on the day of judgment and hear you say: "Come, blessed of my Father, take possession of the kingdom which is prepared for you." We shall praise you, for ever and ever. Amen (Hoosoyo, Prayer of Forgiveness, of Safro, Morning Prayer, Exaltation of the Holy, Life-giving Cross).

The above liturgical texts offer us two models of rich catechesis filled with theology and expressed through biblical imagery. The beautiful and profound statement of the Maronite Evening Prayer, "The cross is the foundation of the Church," is a theme expressed by the fathers, in particular, Cyril of Jerusalem (d. 387) in his lengthy preparation of candidates for baptism and reception into the church.

The Baptismal Catechesis of Cyril of Jerusalem

Cyril's baptismal catechesis was totally dedicated to the cross. Without using difficult theology, Cyril—reflecting his dual position as bishop and catechist—made clear affirmations regarding our redemption and firm exhortations of moral and spiritual character.

In the cross, Cyril saw the fundamental Christian message of salvation that God offers and man accepts. This cross, the instrument of salvation, must be embraced by the Christian. Cyril, who needed no visual aids because he conducted his class on the site of the crucifixion itself, wanted no gray areas about the mystery of salvation. He made the cross a living reality for his catechumens rather than leaving it a mere historical fact (XIII, 4).

This is why Cyril focused on placing the catechumens' faith on the cross: "First therefore, take as an indestructible foundation the Cross, and build upon it the rest of your faith" (XIII, 38). The cross became the unshakable cornerstone of the Christian edifice. The early Christians of Jewish origin, as we see in the Maronite Prayer of Forgiveness of the Morning Prayer, likened the cross to the "Tau," corresponding to our letter T, which was the sign of Yahweh as expressed in Ezekiel (9:4-6). The sign of the cross on the forehead was a sign of consecration to the Lord.

Cyril also explained how the "Tree of Life [the cross] was planted in the earth, to bring blessing for this earth, which has been cursed" (XIII, 35). This is the same thought as expressed in the liturgical prayers above. The cross reveals the triumph and splendor of God because it manifests the love of God that saves humanity, his holy people, making Christ its glorious chief. The bishop-catechist told his listeners that it is the cross of Jesus who unites them (XIII, 40). "The Catholic Church glories in every action of Christ, but the glory of Glories is the Cross" (XIII, 1). The cross became the essential part of life and its activities (XIII, 36).

The Cross As
the Church's Central Mystery

As the paschal mystery of the cross was the focal point for Cyril, so too it remains for the church. From this glorious cross come the graces that constitute the church. Since this glorious cross is the foundation of the church, it underlines my reason for making the beginning of our catechetical liturgical year the season of the Holy Life-giving Cross, the instrument of our salvation. For this reason, before studying this plan of salvation step by step, I think it would be important to see and present it through the praying, worshiping community of the church. This effort will respond to the *Catechism of the Catholic Church*'s invitation to inculturation. Here again the presentation will be founded on the *Catechism* as well as on the liturgy.

The *Catechism of the Catholic Church* presents the church as the mystery/sacrament of salvation for the world. With its roots in Israel, this church is the people of God. "You however are a chosen race, a royal priesthood, a holy nation, a people he claims for his own to proclaim the glorious works of the One who called you from darkness into his marvelous light" (1 Pt 2:9; cf. Ex 19:6). That is how St. Peter refers to the church.

"My mission is only to the lost sheep of the house of Israel," claims Jesus (Mt 15:24; cf. Ez 34). The same mission is entrusted to the disciples: "Go instead after the lost sheep of the house of Israel. As you go, make this announcement, 'The reign of God is at hand!' Cure the sick, raise the dead, heal the leprous, expel demons. The gift you have received, give as a gift" (Mt 10:6-8).

The fulfillment of the messianic promise and of the covenant was addressed to Israel as the People of God (Acts 2:39; 3:25-26). Jews of every background and religious tendency received the Good News that Jesus proclaimed. People were caught between Jesus' messianic signs (Jn 7:31) and the fear of Jerusalem authorities who accused him of leading people astray (Jn 7:12-13). Confronted by Jesus' message, the Pharisees divided along these lines (Jn 9:16-17; 10:19-21), even though some, such as Nicodemus, believed in him (Acts 15:5; 21:20). This same attitude existed among the Sanhedrin (Jn 12:42; 19:38) and, after Pentecost, the "crowd of priests" (Acts 6:7) and Jewish zealots of the Law (Acts 21:20).

The church is not, then, a gathering of a new people of God created to substitute for a rejected Israel. It is rather the same blessing of God on Abraham which unites the pagans (Gal 3:14). There has always been a conflict between the ways of God and human ways. In God's eyes there is one priestly people on earth, even if they gather in different assemblies.

On the one hand, we have a synagogue that looks to God but is blind to the messianic light of Jesus (2 Cor 14-16), seeing itself as guardian of the divine heritage (Lk 15:31) and set apart for the salvation of Gentiles. On the other hand, we have a church in which Jews and pagans are united in Jesus Christ (Ep 2:14-16), with a mission to carry the Good News for the salvation of all nations (Mt 28:19). For God there is only one priestly people who carry his name and message into the world and who are called to offer the sacrifice of the New Covenant.

When the hardened part of Israel is "assumed" into the Messiah (when "the full number of Gentiles enter in" [Rom 11:25]), divine intervention will be "like life coming from death" (Rom 11:15): "If you were cut off from the natural wild olive and, contrary to nature, were grafted into the cultivated olive, so much the more will they who belong to it by nature be grafted into their own olive tree" (Rom 11:24) and "then all Israel will be saved" (Rom 11:26).

The church is "catholic," which in Greek means "universal," "in accord with all," because in it resides the fullness of Christ of whom it is the Body (Eph 1:22). This fullness or plenitude of Christ will not be manifested in glory until the fullness of nations—fullness in the meaning of qualitative rather than quantitative—has entered the church; the fullness of Israel (Rom 11:11) will be "assumed" in him. The church, rooted in the mystery of Israel (Rom 11:25), goes out to all nations, sharing the Good News of universal salvation through Jesus Christ, Son of God, who came into the world as the Messiah of Israel. The *Catechism* describes the church as follows:

> *The church assembles around God's Word and Christ's Body*
>
> 777 The word "Church" means "convocation." It designates the assembly of those whom God's Word "convokes"....

In the church, we will become the assembly of the redeemed

778 The Church is both the means and the goal of God's plan....She will be perfected in the glory of heaven as the assembly of all the redeemed of the earth....

The church's mystery is her human and divine nature

779 The Church is both visible and spiritual, a hierarchical society and the Mystical Body of Christ. She is one, yet formed of two components, human and divine. That is her mystery....

The church is the expression of God's communion with us

780 The Church in this world is the sacrament of salvation, the sign and the instrument of the communion of God and men.

Christ redeemed and purified a people for himself

802 Christ Jesus "gave himself for us to redeem us from all iniquity and to purify for himself a people of his own"....

We are God's chosen people

803 "You are a chosen race, a royal priesthood, a holy nation, God's own people"....

Through faith and baptism we enter Christ's family

804 One enters into the People of God by faith and Baptism. "All men are called to belong to the new People of God"..., so that, in Christ, "men may form one family and one People of God"....

The church is Christ's Body

805 The Church is the Body of Christ. Through the Spirit and his action in the sacraments, above all the Eucharist, Christ, who once was dead and is now risen, establishes the community of believers as his own Body.

Diverse though we are, the Body unites us

806 In the unity of this Body, there is a diversity of members and functions. All members are linked to one another....

Christ heads the Body, his church

807 The Church is this Body of which Christ is the head: she lives from him, in him, and for him; he lives with her and in her.

The church is Christ's bride

808 The Church is the Bride of Christ: he loved her and handed himself over for her.

The church is the Holy Spirit's temple

809 The Church is the Temple of the Holy Spirit. The Spirit is the soul, as it were, of the Mystical Body, the source of its life, of its unity in diversity, and of the riches of its gifts and charisms.

As the Trinity is one, so too the church

810 "Hence the universal Church is seen to be 'a people brought into unity from the unity of the Father, the Son, and the Holy Spirit'"....

The church is for all people and times

868 The Church is catholic: she proclaims the fullness of the faith. She bears in herself and administers the totality of the means of salvation. She is sent out to all peoples. She speaks to all men. She encompasses all times....

In the church we share in holiness

960 The Church is a "communion of saints": this expression refers first to the "holy things" (*sancta*), above all the Eucharist, by which "the unity of believers, who form one body in Christ, is both represented and brought about"....

Whatever one member does affects the others

961 The term "communion of saints" refers also to the communion of "holy persons" (*sancti*) in Christ who "died for all," so that what each one does or suffers in and for Christ bears fruit for all.

The communion of saints embraces earth, purgatory, heaven

962 "We believe in the communion of all the faithful of Christ, those who are pilgrims on earth, the dead who are being purified, and the blessed in heaven, all together forming one Church....

The Church in the Liturgy

I wish to balance these brief summaries taken from the *Catechism* with liturgical prayers that set out the above theological points in a simple, easy-to-understand way. The Roman Rite has a special liturgy called the "Common of the Dedication of a Church," while the Maronite Church starts its liturgical journey, its liturgical year, by celebrating the Sunday of the Consecration of the Church and perhaps at the same time—depending on the number of Sundays between the first Sunday of November and Christmas—the Sunday of the Dedication of the Church. Let us look at some liturgical expressions of the theology and spirituality of moral life.

The church has been built upon a glorious foundation

Roman Rite	Maronite Rite
God our Father, from living stones, your chosen people, you built an eternal temple to your glory. Increase the spiritual gifts you have given to your Church, so that your faithful people may continue to grow into the new and eternal Jerusalem (Opening Prayer, Common of the Dedication of a Church, Anniversary of Dedication).	May we be worthy to render glory, thanksgiving and honor to the wise Architect who, through his grace, constructed his holy Church as fortification of forgiveness and enclosed his priestly people within his care as a stronghold of trust. In his mercy, he built a tower of redemption for his people. Thus, in the community of life, the redeemed ones are protected from all harm by his cross. It is proper to render him praise and honor now and forever. Amen.
Father, you make your Church on earth a sign of the new and eternal Jerusalem. By sharing in this sacrament may we become the temple of your presence and the home of your glory (Prayer after Communion, Common of the Dedication of a Church, Anniversary of Dedication).	O Christ our God, You built that Jerusalem which is known as the holy Church and collected the scattered of Israel within her. The nations confess the saving gospel of him who promised his Church that the gates of hell will not subdue her, neither powers of the earth nor powers above the earth, for God dwells within her lest she tremble. "Behold I am with you to the end of time." The holy prophets foretold of her coming, and the divine apostles preached her redemption. The holy martyrs received a crown because of her true faith.

Roman Rite	**Maronite Rite**
Lord, as we recall the day you filled this church with your glory and holiness, may our lives also become an acceptable offering to you (Prayer over the Gifts, Common of the Dedication of a Church, Anniversary of Dedication).	Because of this, today we celebrate her glorious consecration and say: Arise and shine forth, O holy Church, for the wise Architect who laid your foundations has also constructed the bars of your gates. Arise and shine, because the God who is mighty forevermore chose you as a dwelling place for himself. Arise and shine forth, because he who chooses the living chose life for you until the end of time. Arise and shine forth, because he established your borders in peace, O hope of the ends of the earth.
The streets of Jerusalem will ring with rejoicing; they will resound with the song of praise (Liturgy of the Hours, Antiphon 1, Evening Prayer I, Common of the Dedication of a Church).	Therefore, we petition you, O Lord, and we implore you with the fragrance of this incense to be mindful once again of your Church. In your mercy, redeem the scepter of your inheritance and deliver your flock from adversity. Grant rest to those who have been called from it to your kingdom. In your holy dwellings, grant happiness to those who have served your will and gather them to your right side, to the pleasing aroma of your banquet. Then together, we will render glory to you at all times and for ever. Amen (Hoosoyo, Prayer of Forgiveness, Sunday of the Consecration of the Church).

Roman Rite

Lord,
through these gifts
increase the vision of your truth
   in our minds.
May we always worship you in
   your holy temple,
and rejoice in your presence with
   all your saints
(Prayer after Communion,
Common of the Dedication of a
Church).

This is God's dwelling place and
he has made it holy; here we call
on his name, for Scripture says,
There you will find me (Liturgy of
the Hours, Canticle of Mary,
Evening Prayer II, Common of
the Dedication of a Church).

Your house of prayer
is also the promise of the Church
   in heaven.
Here your love is always at work,
preparing the Church on earth
for its heavenly glory
as the sinless bride of Christ,
the joyful mother of a great
   company of saints
(Preface, Common of the
Dedication of a Church II).

Maronite Rite

May we be worthy to praise,
confess and glorify the One who
renews every generation. For in
his grace, he established the
Church and constantly makes her
new. He summons distant peoples
to her. Within the Church, they
sing fitting praises to him who
existed before the foundations of
the earth. It is, therefore, proper
to render him praise and honor,
now and for ever. Amen.

O Christ our God, Creator and
Establisher of the earth, the
heavens tell of your glory, and the
star-filled firmament shows forth
the work of your hands. Your
power is above, below and
throughout the world. All things
are in you, and you are in all. You
willed to be served by human
hands in an earthly Church.
David foreshadowed the Church
in prophecy, and Isaiah foretold
of her coming in parables.
Through the death of her
Bridegroom, she was betrothed.
Thus was she crowned with
thorns, and through the passion,
she was redeemed. Ornamented
with fine robes, she arose in glory
as a well-appointed palace, a
firmly set city, a fortified tower
and a holy mountain.

Roman Rite	**Maronite Rite**
How safe a dwelling the Lord has made you; how blessed the children within your walls (Liturgy of the Hours, Antiphon 2, Evening Prayer I, Common of the Dedication of a Church).	Therefore, on this joyful day of dedication, we petition you, O Lord, with the fragrance of incense. Look lovingly upon your Church and continually keep her from harm and danger. Confirm her with confidence on the chosen rock of crystal. Mark her children clearly with your redeeming blood. Reassure her with your grace. Gather together her scattered. Strengthen her weak. Visit her poor with the wealth of your compassion. Then, in the assembly of the first-born, she will render glory to you, now and for ever. Amen (Hoosoyo, Prayer of Forgiveness, Sunday of the Dedication of the Church).

Through these passages, we see the Lord is the divine architect who designed the plan of salvation and chose a holy people as his visible instrument to continue this celebration of salvation through their own lives, already living in eternity:

> O Lord, let us walk the straight paths of your divine laws. Grant us to be for you a holy people, a saved gathering and a royal priesthood. May we be worthy to rejoice with all the blessed. We will praise and exalt your most blessed name, with the name of our Lord Jesus Christ and your Holy Spirit, now and for ever (Anaphora of St. James, Teacher of Seroug).

Summary

In this chapter, we have seen how every year the church ("holy people," nourished by "holy things"), enlightened by the vision of the glorious cross of Christ's second coming, journeys with him through the liturgical year. She commemorates his plan of salvation from his first coming, death, resurrection, and ascension into heaven, and awaits his second coming. This plan, these events, are the points we will explore in coming chapters.

Six

God the Father

Glory be to the Father who sent his Son for our
sake; adoration to the Son who, by his crucifixion,
redeemed us; thanksgiving to the Holy Spirit,
through whom the mystery of our salvation was
brought to fullness. Blessed is God who, in his love,
gave us life. To him be glory. Amen (Anaphora,
Maronite Liturgy).

Who is this God, and what is his benevolent plan? Who
and what does this plan involve? The unveiling of
this plan will be presented in two sections: first, as presented
in the *Catechism of the Catholic Church*; second, as it is presented in the Roman and Syriac Maronite liturgies, mainly
during the Sundays preceding Christmas. In the Roman
Church, there are four such Sundays, called collectively the
season of Advent. In the Maronite Church, there are six such
Sundays, each with a particular theme (Announcement to
Zechariah, Mary, and Elizabeth; the Birth of John the Baptizer; the Revelation to Joseph; and Genealogy Sunday),
called collectively the season of Announcements. They prepare us for the greatest announcement, the first coming, the
birth of the Lord Jesus.

In both presentations, we cannot speak of the Father
alone without mentioning the other two Persons, because the

Trinity is unity. After a foretaste of the glory of the second coming to be achieved through a glorious cross, the chosen people, like the three disciples chosen to view the transfiguration, need to take a look at the first coming of Jesus and its advance preparation. He is, after all, the fullness of the revelation. And the way God prepared the world for his coming tells us something about how we should do the same in our catechetical task.

God the Father
in the *Catechism of the Catholic Church*

The *Catechism of the Catholic Church* presents God in the following manner:

"I Am Who Am"

God is "I am who am," the unique principle, transcending the world:

> *He tells us who he is and how to call him*
>
> 206 In revealing his mysterious name, YHWH ("I Am He Who Is," "I Am Who Am," or "I Am Who I Am"), God says who he is and by what name he is to be called. This divine name is mysterious just as God is mystery....
>
> *He reveals his eternal faithfulness*
>
> 207 By revealing his name God at the same time reveals his faithfulness which is from everlasting to everlasting, valid for the past ("I am the God of your fathers"), as for the future....

This existence of God, the church affirms, can be known by natural light of reason, as source and end of all things:

*God can be known as source and destination of the
universe*

32 The *world*: starting from movement, becoming,
contingency, and the world's order and beauty,
one can come to a knowledge of God as the origin
and the end of the universe.

All creatures, including humans, are incomplete and
subject to change. This fact implies the need for a necessary
source of transcendental order. People search for God by
groping (Acts 17:27). God, by revealing himself as YHWH, "I
am who is" (Ex 3:14), shows himself as a principal transcending nature and as a supreme freedom governing human
history in a providential way.

Despite the fact that God reveals himself as the one "Who
is," humans can never have total understanding of God
because he remains "He who dwells in an inaccessible light
which no man has either seen or can see":

God wants to communicate his life and adopt us

52 God, who "dwells in unapproachable light,"
wants to communicate his own divine life to the
men he freely created, in order to adopt them as
his sons in his only-begotten Son....

Also, despite the fact that everything in the world is relative
to God, God is not relative to anything beyond himself
because "with him there exists no change or shadow of
variation":

Israel came to deeper faith in the treasures of God's name

212 Over the centuries, Israel's faith was able to
manifest and deepen realization of the riches
contained in the revelation of the divine name.
God is unique; there are no other gods besides
him....

God's name reveals that he alone exists

213 The revelation of the ineffable name "I Am
who Am" contains then the truth that God alone
IS....

This does not mean that God is inert or passive, but rather it
means that his existence is like the fire which burned the bush
without consuming it (Ex 3:2). This imagery of the fire will
reappear later when we present the text of the annunciation
according to the Syriac Maronite Liturgy.

Eternal Father of the Only Son in the Holy Spirit

God, who is the author of everything but incapable of full
explanation, is the eternal Father of the only Son in the Holy
Spirit. This God, Emmanuel (Mt 1:23), is faithfully engaged
in the covenant that will bring salvation to people through
Jesus in whom God "saves his people from sins":

Jesus' name is full of saving significance

452 The name Jesus means "God saves." The child
born of the Virgin Mary is called Jesus, "for he will
save his people from their sins"....

In Christ Jesus God reconciles the world to himself:

We are saved through God's initiative

620 Our salvation flows from God's initiative of
love for us, because "he loved us and sent his Son
to be the expiation for our sins....

The *Catechism* shows us that it is impossible to speak of
the Father without mentioning the Son or the Spirit. The
liturgy will emphasize this idea more deeply. By embracing
humanity, Jesus becomes the new and final propitiation
(Rom 3:25) and the ultimate high priest who can talk to his
Father as he intensely expresses it in the priestly prayer (Jn
17:6-11), replacing the expiation of Yom Kippur (Lv 16:12-
16) where God's presence in the Holy of Holies cleansed and

forgave people by the blood of the Covenant (Ex 25:17) as the high priest, every year, pronounced the name of YHWH (Ex 34:6):

Jesus was the propitiatory sacrifice

433 The name of the Savior God was invoked only once in the year by the high priest in atonement for the sins of Israel, after he had sprinkled the mercy seat in the Holy of Holies with the sacrificial blood. The mercy seat was the place of God's presence....

God reveals himself to us as Father, by revealing his only Son Jesus Christ, whom he carries in his bosom:

Christian belief in God includes belief in his Son

151 For a Christian, believing in God cannot be separated from believing in the One he sent, his "beloved Son," in whom the Father is "well pleased"; God tells us to listen to him....

This revelation of God the Father through Jesus includes the Holy Spirit, who reveals the "Total Truth":

The Holy Spirit is also a Divine Person

243 Before his Passover, Jesus announced the sending of "another Paraclete" (Advocate), the Holy Spirit. At work since creation, having previously "spoken through the prophets," the Spirit will now be with and in the disciples, to teach them and guide them "into all the truth."....

This Holy Spirit, then, comes from the Father of the Son, Jesus (Jn 16:26), and also from the Son (Gal 4:6). This Spirit, who is different from the Son, glorifies him in being the Spirit of the Father and of the Son in the divine unity (Jn 16:14-15). This Spirit, who was present at the creation, is the Spirit of promise (Jn 3:1-5) who gives us divine life or filial adoption, in Jesus Christ the only Son (Ez 36:27; Rom 8:16). He is the Spirit who spoke through the prophets but who did not reveal himself personally in trinitarian revelation of the divine name until he glorified the Son by the resurrection and Pentecost (Jn 7:39):

> *The Spirit has many titles*
>
> 692 When he proclaims and promises the coming of the Holy Spirit, Jesus calls him the "Paraclete," literally, "he who is called to one's side, *ad-vocatus.* "Paraclete" is commonly translated by "consoler".... The Lord also called the Holy Spirit "the Spirit of truth."
>
> *God wishes to show his love*
>
> 693 Besides the proper name of "Holy Spirit,"...we also find in St. Paul the titles: the Spirit of the promise,...the Spirit of adoption,...the Spirit of Christ,...the Spirit of the Lord...and the Spirit of God—and in St. Peter, the Spirit of glory....

The *Catechism* presents the divine works and the trinitarian missions as follows:

> *God has predestined us in creation*
>
> 257 ...God is eternal blessedness, undying life, unfading light. God is love....God freely wills to communicate the glory of his blessed life. Such is the "plan of his loving kindness," conceived by the Father before the foundation of the world, in his beloved Son....

What we see in the above texts of the *Catechism* is an "All-powerful-God who has an eternal plan for filial adoption" (Eph 1:4-5). So the creation of the world has the plan of God as its foundation (2 Tim 1:9). This predestination does not mean that from the beginning some are saved and others condemned. Rather, it is addressed to all (1 Tm 2:4; 2 Pt 1:4; Rom 8:29). Nor does this predestination mean that there are limits to our freedom to choose. The response of the creature to the Creator will be a response of love that allows not only the person to be divinized but also the surrounding world.

This plan is achieved through Jesus, "the blameless lamb" (1 Pt 1:19-20), who becomes the "first-born of a multitude of brothers" (Rom 8:29).

God's creation, from the invisible world of pure spirits to the visible cosmos, including man created in his image, is part of his plan. It permanently depends on him "in whom we have life, movement and being" (Acts 17:28). God created man and woman and put them in charge:

We are God's stewards in creation

373 In God's plan man and woman have the vocation of "subduing" the earth...as stewards of God....God calls man and woman,...to share in his providence toward other creatures....

Man, created according to a divine filial adoption, because he was created free, was able to choose. Even though from the beginning a loving relationship existed between God and man, man's continual loving response was to be the product of his free will. This choice of continual loving response needed total trusting abandonment to the Father. In this relationship between God and man, God is the one who remains faithful, despite our unfaithfulness; he "stays faithful because he cannot deny himself (2 Tm 2:13).

God is the one who remained faithful as he prepared the salvation of humanity in its entirety, which he promised from the original fall (3:15). Renewing this covenant with Abraham, Isaac, and Jacob and through kings, prophets, and priests, God prepared the scattered people for the ultimate messianic renewal of the covenant which, through Christ, the suffering servant, will be made eternal as the "covenant of the people and light of all nations":

The Law could be fulfilled only by Jesus

580 The perfect fulfillment of the Law could be the work of none but the divine legislator, born subject to the Law in the person of the Son....In Jesus, the Law no longer appears engraved on tables of stone but "upon the heart" of the Servant who becomes

"a covenant to the people," because he will
"faithfully bring forth justice.".....

God the Father in Liturgical Tradition

Having briefly sketched what the *Catechism* tells us about
God the Father, I wish to present how the early Syriac
Maronite Church reflects the same teachings through the
Sunday liturgy, beginning with the Sundays of the Announcements mentioned above, preparing for the first coming of Jesus Christ, the fulfillment of the New Covenant. The
Roman Rite has no such corresponding Sundays, instead
tracing over the four-week season of Advent salvation history
going well back into the Old Testament.

In the Maronite liturgy, in the Anaphora of St. James,
"brother of the Lord," right before the words of institution,
we read:

Jesus came to renew God's image in the world

Roman Rite	Maronite Rite
Father, all-powerful and ever-living God, we do well always and everywhere to give you thanks through Jesus Christ our Lord.	Holy are you, King of earth and Source of life. Holy is your only-begotten Son, Jesus Christ, and holy is your Spirit who dwells in all creation. In the beginning, you formed man from the earth in your image and gave him the
His future coming was proclaimed by all the prophets. The virgin mother bore him in her womb with love beyond all telling. John the Baptist was his herald and made him known when at last he came (Eucharistic Prayer, Advent II).	joy of paradise. When he transgressed your command, you did not reject him, but called him back by the law as a merciful Father. You guided him by the prophets. And the time was fulfilled, you sent your Son into the world, that he might renew

Roman Rite	Maronite Rite
	your image. He became man by the Holy Spirit and the Virgin Mary and accomplished all things for the salvation of our race (Anaphora of St. James).

This is only a short summary of the loving Father and his plan of salvation. We will give more details about how the Syriac Maronite Tradition reflects what was expressed in the *Catechism of the Catholic Church*. The name of God "I am who am" is used in the ceremony of exorcism before baptism:

We cast out the devil by God's name

Roman Rite	Maronite Rite
	I exorcise you, wicked demons and unclean spirits, and all the army of the enemy, in the fearsome name + of God who creates and provides for all, who sits on the chariot of crystal, and is served by thousands and before whom stand myriads of myriads.

I exorcise you, in the great and fearsome name of "I am who am," + the mighty God and Lord of the armies, who spoke to Moses from the bush and came down to Sinai, with the sound of trumpets. I exorcise you, in the wonderful, ever-reigning name, of God almighty, + who became man and |

Roman Rite	Maronite Rite
	vanquished your dominion, who humbled himself by his own will, embraced death on the wooden cross, and redeemed Adam and his children from the slavery of sin.
	I exorcise you, to depart from this creature, betrothed to the living God, + to disperse and leave alone this servant of God, who came to be a dwelling place of the Holy Spirit.
	Behold the shepherd runs toward his lamb! When he sees the ravening wolf, he will destroy it, like the cloud at the approach of the wind. And I sign and seal this lamb against the power of the devils, in the name of the + Father, and of the + Son, and of the + Holy Spirit (Prayer of Exorcism, Baptismal Ceremony).

This God the Father is expressed in the Prayer of Forgiveness of the feast of Pentecost in the following manner:

We ask the all-powerful God for salvation in the Spirit

Roman Rite	Maronite Rite
	May we be worthy to praise, confess and glorify the hidden

Roman Rite	Maronite Rite
	One who is beyond human thought, understanding and perception. He exists of himself, knows himself and is sufficient unto himself. He creates, supports and rules the visible and invisible. Likewise, he is without beginning and continues without end. He is eternal and incomprehensible, one equal power, one will, shared harmoniously by the Father, Son and Holy Spirit, in whom there is no title or person who is before or after another. Glory and honor are due to him, for ever. Amen.

O hidden and incomprehensible God, everlasting and infinite, you are known in a single essence and are adorned by Three Holy Persons. You exist in three proper characteristics in knowable and reasonable natures, yet you are one God, known in Three Holy Persons, a perfect Trinity, made up of Three Perfect Beings, the Father, the Son, and the Holy Spirit. O God the Father, You deigned to create man in your image, but through his evil will, he went astray to the worship of demons. You sent your Son, the Word, from your inscrutable depths. He became a man and without change,

Roman Rite	Maronite Rite
	communicated with us plainly and explained the mystery of God. He made us understand what could not be understood. He also taught us about the third light of Godhead which ineffably proceeds from you: the Spirit of wisdom, of might and of knowledge; the perfecting Spirit; the pure and imponderable Spirit; the Spirit, lover of all people; the Spirit, foundation of prophets, wisdom of apostles, sustenance of martyrs and guide of teachers; the Spirit benefactor; the omnipotent Spirit; the Spirit, source of divine gifts; the Spirit, simple in his nature; the Spirit whose nature and rank in the heavenly kingdom are equal to you and to your Son; the Spirit who is close to all, fills all and consecrates all with his power.
Holy Father, send your Spirit to us who know not how to pray as we ought, that he may help us in our frailty, and ask for us those gifts which will make us pleasing to you.	Therefore, we petition you on this glorious day of the holy feast of Pentecost, upon which you hovered over the holy apostles: stretch forth your merciful right hand over your worshipers and servants and fill us all with the richness of your divine favors. Through your power, confer upon us your holy gifts and uproot from your children of grace all weakness and feebleness
Christ, Son of the living God, you asked the Father to send the Holy Spirit upon your Church, make us worthy to have this Spirit of Truth with us always.	

Roman Rite	**Maronite Rite**
Come, Holy Spirit, that we may show your fruit in our lives, charity, joy, peace, equanimity, kindness, generosity, long-suffering, patience, faithfulness, modesty, self-control, chastity.	of sin. Establish us as holy sanctuaries for your habitation. Free us and make us impregnable to the violent onslaught of our enemies. Grant a kind memory and joyful resurrection to all the faithful departed, children of the Church. You reign upon us,
Father all-powerful, you have sent the Spirit of your Son into our hearts, so that we cry: Abba, Father, make us submissive to your Spirit, that we may be your heirs, and coheirs with Christ (Liturgy of the Hours, Intercessions, Morning Prayer, Pentecost).	Father, Lord of all, with your Son who renews all and your blissful and life-giving Spirit who perfects all, now and for ever. Amen (Hoosoyo, Prayer of Forgiveness, Pentecost).

This loving God executed his plan of salvation in a way that became accessible to his children. Preparation for carrying out this plan would be necessary. It would occur by means of various persons He selected throughout history, mainly by John the Forerunner. In the following liturgical texts is summarized the entire history of salvation:

Announcement to Zechariah

John, the subject of this announcement, is to be given the beautiful name meaning "God is gracious [to his people]": "You-hanon." He will become the one we know as John the Baptizer or Forerunner. This occasion is expressed in the Syriac Maronite Liturgy in the following words:

We ask God to come again as throughout Israel's history

Roman Rite	Maronite Rite
Zechariah entered the temple of the lord, and the angel Gabriel appeared to him, standing on the right of the altar of incense (Liturgy of the Hours, Canticle of Mary, Evening Prayer I, Birth of John the Baptist).	May we be worthy to praise, confess and glorify the Almighty Lord who spoke to Adam in the garden. He guided his chosen ones through the desert and appeared to prophets and apostles under various forms. He sent an angel to await Zechariah's ministry in the temple, and there he revealed to him the coming of the forerunner. For this Lord, it is proper to render praise and honor, now and for ever. Amen.

O Lord of heaven and earth, in times past, you spoke to your chosen ones through messengers and angels. Adam heard you walking through the garden, and your voice led Abraham to a strange and new land. Moses saw you in a cloud and in a pillar of fire. Your mysterious words appeared, traced on the wall by an unknown hand. Through these means, you have prepared a straight and level path for the final revealer of your mystery. You have spoken, yet you have no mouth. You have no feet, yet you have led. You have never known sin, but you are infinite in your mercy toward sinners.

Roman Rite	Maronite Rite
	Now, on this day of the announcement of John, forerunner of the Lord, we approach you amid clouds of incense with the hope of gaining a kind hearing, look with kindness upon a wayward people and an obstinate nation. Come once more with the announcement of the forerunner and send us another angel of good news. Then, reassured of your compassion, we will praise you, now and for ever. Amen (Hoosoyo, Prayer of Forgiveness, Sunday of the Announcement to Zechariah).

After the Announcement of the Forerunner, it would be natural to unveil the one for whom the way is being prepared, the Lord Jesus.

Announcement to Mary

Like Mary, we stand uncomprehending at God's coming

Roman Rite	Maronite Rite
A flower has sprung from Jesse's stock, and a star has risen from Jacob....The Virgin has given birth to the Savior, and a star has risen from Jacob. Glory to the Father and the Son and the Holy Spirit. (Liturgy of the Hours, Responsory, Evening Prayer I, Annunciation).	May we be worthy to praise and confess the God of earth and sky, the Creator, the Sustainer, the Life-Giver. In his love and fore-knowledge, he decided to return to the heirs of Adam and pitch his tent in their midst. Prophets, apostles and teachers

Roman Rite

Maronite Rite

came before him in order to create a well-disposed people. Finally, the "Man of God," Gabriel, came and revealed his imminent coming. To the God of this holy dispensation, we offer praise and thanksgiving, now and for ever. Amen.

You chose the Virgin Mary as the mother of your Son, have mercy on all who look for your gift of salvation. You sent Gabriel to give Mary your message of peace and joy, give to the whole world the joy of salvation and your gift of true peace. Mary gave her consent, the Holy Spirit overshadowed her, and your Word came to dwell among us, touch our hearts that we may welcome Christ as Mary did (Liturgy of the Hours, Intercessions, Evening Prayer I, Annunciation).

With fear and amazement, the Virgin Mary received the angel messenger. "Peace be with you, Mary. The Lord is with you. Blessed are you among all women." Mary answered, "Never have I heard such greeting. Who are you; who is your Lord, and why have you come?" "I am Gabriel. My name means 'God's Strong One', and I have come to tell you that you will bear a son, Immanuel, by the overshadowing of God's own Holy Spirit." Mary was overtaken with wonder and astonishment. Fear seized her, and doubt filled her mind. "Good sir, I am but a girl. Do not speak to me this way." The angel said, "Mary, the power of God's Spirit is now upon you. Your son is the long-awaited hope of the prophets. He dwells in eternal realms, and fiery ranks of angels accompany him, for he is the flaming Word of God, a searing fire, a white hot coal." Mary said,

Roman Rite	Maronite Rite
	"I am a mortal creature. Surely I will be consumed by God's all-consuming fire. How fearful is this moment! How my breath leaves me for fear! How humble am I, and how overcome that such a thing should come to pass!"
Almighty Father of our Lord Jesus Christ, you have revealed the beauty of your power by exalting the lowly virgin of Nazareth and making her the mother of our Savior. May the prayers of this woman bring Jesus to the waiting world and fill the void of incompletion with the presence of her child, who lives and reigns with you and the Holy Spirit, one God, for ever and ever (Alternative Opening Prayer, Annunciation).	Now, O Lord, we are seized with amazement, and like Mary, we do not understand. With her we draw back, blinded by your eternal Flame, scorched by its touch and overcome by its power. We know only to offer incense as a fitting response to so great a Word who this day makes his presence among us. Behind clouds of perfumed smoke, we cower and dare not even glimpse the power that now descends over our altar. Purge us with your living Flame, O God. Treat us as wayward children and not as hostile enemies. And we will praise you, now and for ever. Amen (Hoosoyo, Prayer of Forgiveness, Sunday of the Announcement to Mary).

Visitation to Elizabeth

These two subjects of announcement, John and Jesus, are soon to meet. Mary, knowing of her cousin Elizabeth's pregnancy, goes to help, for her life is one of service:

God has worked miracles through his chosen woman

Roman Rite	**Maronite Rite**
Let us glorify our Savior, who chose the Virgin Mary for his mother....Sun of Justice, the immaculate Virgin was the white dawn announcing your rising, grant that we may always live in the light of your coming (Liturgy of the Hours, Intercessions, Morning Prayer, Visitation).	May we be worthy to praise, confess and glorify the Lord of all eternity who hid himself in the womb of a virgin. The Ancient of Days who was concealed in the virgin's temple; the everlasting God who joined heaven and earth by communing with a simple maiden. It is proper to render praise and honor to him, now and for ever. Amen.
Mary arose and went with haste into the hill country, to a town of Judah.

When Elizabeth heard Mary's greeting, the infant in her womb leaped for joy, and she was filled with the Holy Spirit (Liturgy of the Hours, Antiphons 1 and 2, Morning Prayer, Visitation). | O God, your name was before the ages, and you have no beginning. Within a virgin's womb, you chose to make your abode with all people. With your mother, Mary, you traveled to visit the aged Elizabeth, and she rejoiced at your coming. In the past, you sent Ruth to Naomi with the news of the Savior's appearance. Naomi rejoiced, for the long awaited Lord dwelt within her house. You did not leave Naomi in the strange land of Moab, but you led her to the safe haven of Bethlehem, to the home of her relatives and friends. To Mary, you brought the news of the miraculous conception of Elizabeth in her old age, and Mary hastened to the hill country |

Roman Rite

Maronite Rite

to abide with Elizabeth as you abided in the womb of Mary. You who were on a mountain, and would appear again on a mountain with Moses and Elias, were concealed by the hills and mountains of Judea. Your mother went quickly to the dwelling of Elizabeth, and you accompanied her, for the tops of the mountains were your dwelling place from the beginning of times. As Elizabeth's child leapt for joy at your coming, so did the mountains and hills leap and jump for joy as their Creator descended to dwell upon them.

Blessed are you, Mary, because you believed that the Lord's words to you would be fulfilled (Liturgy of the Hours, Antiphon 3, Morning Prayer, Visitation).

Today, O Lord, in the company of Mary and Elizabeth, we approach your mountain dwelling. We remove our shoes as did Moses, but we are still unworthy. With confidence in your mercy, we offer our incense to you and say: Blessed is the fruit of the virgin's womb! Blessed is she who trusted that the Lord's word to her would be fulfilled! Blessed are the feet of Mary who brought the hope of ages to Elizabeth and to all people! Glory to You, O Lord, now and for ever. Amen (Hoosoyo, Prayer of Forgiveness, Sunday of the Visitation of Mary to Elizabeth).

The visitation is also expressed in the Prayer of Forgiveness of the Evening and Morning Prayers of the feast.

With the angels, we proclaim God's praise for his salvation

Roman Rite	**Maronite Rite**
	Praise, glory and honor to the Most High, who fills the heavens with glory and pours out his loving kindness upon the earth. The cherubim fear him when they bear him on the fiery chariot but in his love he concealed himself within the pure womb of Mary; he filled his Forerunner John, with the Holy Spirit when he was still in the womb of his mother. The Good One, is due glory and honor this evening, and all the days of our lives, now and for ever. Amen.
May we always recognize with joy the presence of Christ in the Eucharist we celebrate, as John the Baptist hailed the presence of our Savior in the womb of Mary (Prayer after Communion, Visitation).	Glory to you, eternal Child begotten of the Father before all ages. In the fullness of time you took flesh in the womb of the Virgin Mary. You are the King of kings who crowns princes and saves his people. You raised our human nature to the throne of your glory when you descended from that throne, took the condition of a slave and truly became man. Our Spirit is not able to comprehend this humility and our tongue is unable to

Roman Rite

Maronite Rite

describe it. When you placed
yourself within the womb of the
Virgin, she went to the hills of
Judea where she met John, still in
the womb of Elizabeth. She
delighted in him with the gift of
the Holy Spirit and filled the
mountain with joy.

O God, worker of miracles, you
made the Immaculate Virgin
Mary share body and soul in your
Son's glory in heaven, direct the
hearts of your children to that
same glory....You crowned Mary
queen of heaven, may all the
dead rejoice in your kingdom
with the saints for ever (Liturgy of
the Hours, Intercessions, Evening
Prayer, Visitation).

And now, with the angels and all
your people, we proclaim: "Praise
the Lord our God, praise him for
ever." We entreat you with your
Forerunner: pour your mercy
upon us and assist us with your
strength; enlighten us with your
teaching and guide us. Then shall
we go forth to meet you and be
seated at your table, dressed in
our wedding garments. May the
living and the dead be seated one
day at your right hand in the
heavenly dwellings. And we shall
give glory to you, your father, and
your Holy Spirit now and for
ever. Amen (Prayer of
Forgiveness, Evening Prayer).

Roman Rite

You are our redeemer, who made the immaculate Virgin Mary your purest home and the sanctuary of the Holy Spirit, make us temples of your Spirit forever (Liturgy of the Hours, Intercessions, Morning Prayer, Visitation).

Maronite Rite

Praise, glory and honor to the true God whose Spirit one cannot fathom and upon whose face one cannot gaze. He alone possesses perfect knowledge and full comprehension, and the creator of all things seen and unseen, without beginning or end. To the Good One is due glory and honor this morning, and all the days of our lives, now and for ever. Amen.

You who dwell in the heights and are served by seraphim and glorified by the cherubim, descended from your heavens and came to us. In the house of Zechariah you poured your grace upon your Forerunner. On this day, the words of the prophet are fulfilled: "Rejoice, O Mount Zion, and leap with joy, O hills of Judea." On this day, Elizabeth rejoiced and sings: "Come in peace, burning bush of Moses, fleece of Gideon, lamp of the sanctuary of Zechariah. In peace, full of grace, you are blessed among women and blessed is the fruit of your womb."

Roman Rite	Maronite Rite
Eternal Father, you inspired the Virgin Mary, mother of your Son, to visit Elizabeth and assist her in her need. Keep us open to the working of your Spirit, and with Mary may we praise you for ever. We ask this through our Lord Jesus Christ, your Son, who lives and reigns with you and the Holy Spirit, one God, for ever and ever (Opening Prayer, Visitation).	May we commemorate this wonderful feast with spiritual hymns, asking you, O Word of God, by our incense (prayer) to grant us your grace, enlighten us with your light, and strengthen us in the true faith. May our joy bring us to you and may we desire to meet you with all our heart. All of us, the living and the dead will give glory to you, your Father, and your Holy Spirit, now and for ever. Amen (Prayer of Forgiveness, Morning Prayer).

Birth of John the Baptizer

John was announced, but this announcement is to be achieved. This is how the achievement is expressed in several contexts:

John the Baptist tells of God's salvation

Roman Rite	Maronite Rite
Let us pray joyfully to God our Father who called John the Baptist to proclaim the coming of the kingdom of Christ: *O Lord, guide our feet into the way of peace...* (Liturgy of the Hours, Intercessions, Evening Prayer, Beheading of John the Baptist, Martyr).	May we be worthy to praise, confess and extol the Son, the eternal Word. His Father has sent to us the messenger of his coming to prepare the way for his birth in the flesh. Let us magnify the Godhead whose divine and imponderable plan is announced

105

Roman Rite

Maronite Rite

this day by the birth of John the Baptizer. Glory and worship to the good One, for today infinity breaks the barrier of our world and fills it with the news of an astounding birth. Let us magnify him, now and for ever. Amen.

God our Father, the voice of John the Baptist challenges us to repentance and points the way to Christ the Lord.

Open our ears to his message, and free our hearts to turn from our sins and receive the life of the gospel (Alternative Opening Prayer, Birth of John the Baptist).

We listen attentively to your announcement, O Baptizer. We gather at the banks of the river of mercy and impatiently await the One of whom you speak. O John, child of wonder, you came to your parents in their old age, and your miraculous birth is your first sign to us. For One is coming whose birth will make the heavens shake and whose appearance will make the earth tremble. Therefore we cry out and say: O voice preaching in the wilderness, fill the wilderness of our poor lives with your happy announcement. O forerunner of the Word of God, hurry to us who stand like bewildered and lost children in the hope of being found. O John, child of wonder, infant of grace, grace us with the message for which our souls long: the Savior is coming soon. He shall not delay! Praise be to him for ever. Amen (Hoosoyo, Prayer of Forgiveness, Sunday of the Birth of John the Baptizer).

We praise God's work in John the Baptist

Roman Rite	Maronite Rite
In faith let us call upon Christ who sent John to prepare for his coming: *Dawn from on high, break upon us* (Liturgy of the Hours, Intercessions, Morning Prayer, Beheading of John the Baptist, Martyr).	Praise, glory and honor to the Son, the Eternal Word, the Ray of the eternal Father; before his incarnation he sent his messenger to prepare his way. To the Good One is due glory and honor this evening and all the days of our lives. Now and for ever. Amen.
You called John the Baptizer from his mother's womb to prepare the way of your Son, help us to follow in that path which the Baptist opened before the Lord Jesus.	To you we sing praise today, Messenger, Forerunner, and Baptizer. You are the child announced by the angel of God. You are the voice crying in the desert, the prophet who—while still in the womb—knew the
May your Church, in imitation of the Baptist, fearlessly point out the Lamb of God, so that people in every age may acknowledge that the Lord comes to them (Liturgy of the Hours, Intercessions, Evening Prayer I, Birth of John the Baptist).	mystery of the Lord. You are the Middle Covenant, bringing to an end the old law and inaugurating the new. You are the greatest among the children of women, who announced the Most High. You are the Announcer, born of a barren woman to witness to the child born of the Virgin. O child of a priest of the Lord, sign of God's Mercy and apostle of the kingdom of peace, you are the star pointing out the true Light coming into the world, the moon encircling the eternal sun. You are the Messenger of the Lord, the beacon of churches and

Roman Rite	Maronite Rite
	monasteries (Evening Prayer, Sunday of the Birth of John the Baptizer).
You called John the Baptist to give testimony to you by his life and even by his death, help us to imitate his unceasing witness to your truth (Liturgy of the Hours, Intercessions, Evening Prayer, Beheading of John the Baptist, Martyr).	Today, Zechariah rejoices and his tongue is unbound. Today, Elizabeth, whose long wait has come to an end, gives thanks. Today, every mountain leaps for joy. We beseech you, prophet of the Most High, obtain for us from your Lord his grace which works wonders, that our souls may be adorned with good works and that we may witness to the true faith. With Zechariah, your father, and Elizabeth, your mother, we give thanks to the son you desired to see while still in the womb. We shall praise the Father, who made you a messenger of his beloved Son, and glorify the Holy Spirit, with which you were filled before your birth. Glory to the Holy Trinity for ever. Amen (Prayer of Forgiveness, Evening Prayer).

Revelation to Joseph

Despite the announcements from heaven, the human mind has difficulty comprehending these mysteries. Joseph exemplifies struggling humanity trying to balance the human and the divine. That is how the revelation to Joseph becomes an announcement preparing us for the greatest announcement of all: the birth of the Lord. It is a complicated situation to grasp, but our Maronite liturgy finds a beautiful way of expressing it so that we can more easily understand: "The heart of Joseph was in God. A light rose from his heart and revealed the mystery in a dream" (Mazmooro, Sunday of the Revelation to Joseph).

We praise God while recalling Joseph's great role

Roman Rite	Maronite Rite
God of all righteousness, you want us all to be like you, may Saint Joseph inspire us to walk always in your way of holiness (Liturgy of the Hours, Intercessions, Evening Prayer 1, Joseph, Husband of Mary).	May we be worthy to praise, confess and glorify the glorious Son who sent the angel Gabriel to righteous Joseph; the eternal Light who dwelt in the womb of the pure virgin; the Good One to whom are due glory and honor on this day and all the days of our lives and for ever. Amen.
God, in your infinite wisdom and love you chose Joseph to be the husband of Mary, the mother of your Son. May we have the help of his prayers in heaven and enjoy his protection on earth (Opening Prayer, St. Joseph, Votive Mass).	Is there any lofty place like yours, O honorable and righteous Joseph? You served the Lord and his mother and were their constant companion both day and night. You carried on your arm the One who supports all people. You spoke with the eternal Word, and you were the guardian of his mother, the blessed Virgin, betrothed to you in purity. O mystery of Jacob realized! O true and perfect dream come true! How blessed are you among the saints and how honorable among virgins! For this reason we cry out and say: Hail to you, O blessed

Roman Rite	**Maronite Rite**
	angel, who accompanied the Savior and defended him from all misfortune! Hail to you, O virgin who cared for the Virgin, the daughter of the Father and the spouse of the Holy Spirit! Hail to you, O luminous star in the heavenly Church! You guide her children along the right path.
You chose Joseph the righteous to care for your Son in childhood and youth, teach us to care for Christ's body by caring for our brothers and sisters (Liturgy of the Hours, Intercessions, Morning Prayer, Joseph, Husband of Mary).	O innocent and righteous Joseph, we now petition you with the clouds of incense that we raise: intercede for us with the Lord whom you served throughout your life. Implore him to watch over us in this world and keep us from the misfortune of soul and body. And we will glorify the Holy, life-giving Trinity, now and for ever. Amen (Hoosoyo, Prayer of Forgiveness, Sunday of the Revelation to Joseph).

We praise God through Joseph and Mary

Roman Rite	**Maronite Rite**
All-holy Father, you revealed to Saint Joseph your eternal plan of salvation in Christ, deepen our understanding of your Son, true God and true man (Liturgy of the Hours, Intercessions, Evening	Praise, glory and honor to the Most High, who adorned his creatures with gifts and their offspring with the beauty of his wisdom. He revealed to Joseph that Mary had conceived in all

Roman Rite

Prayer I, Joseph, Husband of
Mary).

Maronite Rite

purity the only Son, and through
the voice of the angel Gabriel told
him that the child was to be the
Son of the heavenly Father. To
the Good One is due glory and
honor this evening, and the days
of our lives, now and for ever.
Amen.

O God, you are the beginning
and the end of all feasts and give
meaning to them. When you saw
that those you created for your
praise had strayed and gone away
from you, you became incarnate
in order to save them and allow
them to celebrate a perpetual
feast with you. Today we celebrate
the memory of your divine
revelation which dispelled
Joseph's turmoil and enabled him
to believe that the child had been
conceived by the Holy Spirit. We
thank you for having protected
the Virgin, the pure one among
all who are pure, from any
suspicion or accusation.

Lord, we beseech you, through
the intercession of Mary, your
Mother and Joseph your chosen
one, to mercifully accept our
prayer. May this feast be for our
salvation, may every sinner be
sanctified, all trials pass and all
doubts cease. May the one who is

Roman Rite	Maronite Rite
	far away return and the one who is near be protected. May peace and joy be poured out in this world and love and unity win hearts. May the souls of the departed find rest in the dwelling places of joy. We shall give you glory, now and for ever. Amen (Hoosoyo, Prayer of Forgiveness, Evening Prayer).

Genealogy Sunday

The last Sunday of these Announcements is the day on which the predecessors of Jesus are remembered, as we join our hearts with the faith of the holy fathers of old who awaited the coming of the Lord through the ages.

We praise God for sending Jesus into the world

Roman Rite	Maronite Rite
Lord God, may we, your people, who look forward to the birthday of Christ experience the joy of salvation and celebrate that feast with love and thanksgiving. We ask this through our Lord Jesus Christ, your Son, who lives and reigns with you and the Holy Spirit, one God, for ever and ever (Liturgy of the Hours, Prayer, Evening Prayer, Sunday of the Third Week of Advent).	May we be worthy to praise, glorify and honor the Ancient of Days who is eternally begotten of the Father and was in due time born of a virgin; the light and image of the Father who is One Being with the Father. By his birth, the sayings of the prophets have been fulfilled. To the Good One are due glory and honor on this feast day and all the days of our lives and for ever. Amen.

Roman Rite

Father, all-powerful and
  ever-living God,
we do well always and everywhere
  to give you thanks
through Jesus Christ our Lord.

Today you fill our hearts with joy
as we recognize in Christ the
  revelation of your love.
No eye can see his glory as our
  God,
yet now he is seen as one like us.

Christ is your Son before all ages,
yet now he is born in time
(Eucharistic Prayer, Christmas II).)

In his love Christ has filled us
  with joy
as we prepare to celebrate his
  birth,
so that when he comes he may
  find us watching in prayer,
our hearts filled with wonder and
  praise:

And so, with all the choirs of
  angels in heaven
we proclaim your glory
and join in their unending hymn
of praise...
(Eucharistic Prayer, Advent II).

Maronite Rite

Glory to you, O only Son! You are
without beginning or end, yet you
willed to be born as a child in due
time. O great and almighty One,
you became man with no change
in your divinity. O hidden
mystery, you were seen in human
form while your secret thoughts
were not revealed to those who
see. O Child, the Ancient of Days,
wrapped in swaddling clothes, the
shepherds of Bethlehem and the
Magi of the East prepared to go
and worship you. The angels of
heaven gathered and sang:
"Glory to God in the highest, and
on earth, peace."

Now with joy and happiness, the
Church on earth prepares for
your nativity. Grant that all voices
may be joined together in a song
of exaltation, so we may welcome
your feast with joy. We glorify
you, your Father and your Holy
Spirit, now and for ever. Amen
(Hoosoyo, Prayer of Forgiveness,
Genealogy Sunday).

This is how the message of God the Father and his plan for humanity are expressed and taught in the liturgy. It would be possible to search in each of these prayers for the biblical references contained, without which these prayers could not exist, and for the addressing of the threefold concerns of who God is, who we are, and who we ought to be. Each prayer could become a rich resource for members of a family or class as a communal evening prayer.

Summary

The *Catechism* shows us the uniqueness of God and his fatherhood in many exquisite dimensions of his love. In turn we have seen how the liturgy develops these same themes. This is the first set of parallels between catechism and liturgy, as we will see when we move on to look at the way the Son and the Holy Spirit are also delineated in these two sources.

Seven

God the Son

The *Catechism of the Catholic Church* and the liturgy have much to tell about who Jesus is. Both draw deeply on the events of his life.

God the Son
in the *Catechism of the Catholic Church*

The *Catechism* tells us that Christ is the very heart of catechesis itself.

Catechesis is to bring people into communion with Jesus

426 "At the heart of catechesis we find, in essence, a Person, the Person of Jesus of Nazareth, the only Son from the Father....To catechize is "to reveal in the Person of Christ the whole of God's eternal design reaching fulfillment in that Person. It is to seek to understand the meaning of Christ's actions and words and of the signs worked by him." Catechesis aims at putting "people...in communion...with Jesus Christ: only he can lead us to the love of the Father in the Spirit and make us share in the life of the Holy Trinity."

Christ is the subject matter of catechesis

427 In catechesis "Christ, the Incarnate Word and Son of God,...is taught—everything else is taught with reference to him—and it is Christ alone who teaches—anyone else teaches to the extent that he is Christ's spokesman....

Since Christ is the center of our catechesis, we should summarize the main events of his salvific life: his birth, life, death, and resurrection. Jesus Christ is the eternal Son of God who became man and the Messiah of Israel, giving filial adoption to all those predestined by the divine plan, children of Abraham.

The Incarnation

Jesus was obedient even to the point of death

461 [T]he Church calls "Incarnation" the fact that the Son of God assumed a human nature in order to accomplish our salvation in it....he humbled himself and became obedient unto death, even death on a cross....

Christian faith centers on the incarnation

463 Belief in the true Incarnation of the Son of God is the distinctive sign of Christian faith: "By this you know the Spirit of God"....

God fulfilled his promise of descendants to Abraham

706 Against all human hope, God promises descendants to Abraham, as the fruit of faith and of the power of the Holy Spirit....

God sent Jesus to redeem us in his own time

422 "But when the time had fully come, God sent forth his Son, born of a woman, born under the law, to redeem those who were under the law, so that we might receive adoption as sons."...

The historical Jesus is God's Son

423 We believe and confess that Jesus of Nazareth, born a Jew of a daughter of Israel at Bethlehem at the time of King Herod the Great and the emperor Caesar Augustus, a carpenter by trade, who died crucified in Jerusalem under the procurator Pontius Pilate during the reign of the emperor Tiberius, is the eternal Son of God made man....

The Circumcision

The birth of Jesus is the beginning of the mystery of his infancy. It begins with the circumcision:

Circumcision made Jesus a descendant of Abraham

527 Jesus' *circumcision*, on the eighth day after his birth,...is the sign of his incorporation into Abraham's descendants, into the people of the covenant.....

Epiphany and Baptism

Epiphany shows Jesus as Israel's Messiah

528 The *Epiphany* is the manifestation of Jesus as Messiah of Israel, Son of God and Savior of the world. The great feast of Epiphany celebrates the adoration of Jesus by the wise men (*magi*) from the East, together with his baptism in the Jordan and the wedding feast at Cana in Galilee....

Jesus' baptism shows his acceptance of his earthly mission

536 The baptism of Jesus is on his part the acceptance and inauguration of his mission as God's suffering Servant. He allows himself to be numbered among sinners; he is already "the Lamb of God, who takes away the sin of the world."....

We are immolated with Jesus in baptism

537 Through Baptism the Christian is sacramentally assimilated to Jesus, who in his own baptism anticipates his death and resurrection....

The Finding in the Temple

A story of Jesus' full availability to the Father is all we know of his childhood

534 The *finding of Jesus in the temple* is the only event that breaks the silence of the Gospels about the hidden years of Jesus....Here Jesus lets us catch a glimpse of the mystery of his total consecration to a mission that flows from his divine sonship: "Did you not know that I must be about my Father's work?"....

Jesus esteemed the Temple

583 Like the prophets before him Jesus expressed the deepest respect for the Temple in Jerusalem....

Jesus' Public Life

Cana begins Mary's role of intercession with Jesus

2618 The Gospel reveals to us how Mary prays and intercedes in faith. At Cana...the mother of Jesus asks her son for the needs of a wedding feast....

We are given to Mary's maternal concern

2674 Mary gave her consent in faith at the Annunciation and maintained it without hesitation at the foot of the Cross. Ever since, her motherhood has extended to the brothers and sisters of her Son "who still journey on earth...."

There are many proofs of Jesus' Messiahship

547 Jesus accompanies his words with many "mighty works and wonders and signs," which

manifest that the kingdom is present in him and attest that he was the promised Messiah....

These signs invite our faith

548 The signs worked by Jesus attest that the Father has sent him. They invite belief in him....To those who turn to him in faith, he grants what they ask....So miracles strengthen faith in the One who does his Father's works; they bear witness that he is the Son of God....

The greatest of Jesus' miracles is freedom from sin

549 By freeing some individuals from the earthly evils of hunger, injustice, illness, and death...Jesus performed messianic signs. Nevertheless he did not come to abolish all evils here below...but to free men from the gravest slavery, sin....

Jesus' ability to forgive sins was a stumbling block

589 Jesus gave scandal above all when he identified his merciful conduct toward sinners with God's own attitude toward them....By forgiving sins Jesus either is blaspheming as a man who made himself God's equal or is speaking the truth, and his person really does make present and reveal God's name....

Jesus was the Suffering Servant

601 The Scriptures had foretold this divine plan of salvation through the putting to death of "the righteous one, my Servant" as a mystery of universal redemption, that is, as the ransom that would free men from the slavery of sin....

Weight of sin made Jesus feel intense separation from God

603 ...[H]e assumed us in the state of our waywardness of sin, to the point that he could say in our name from the cross: "My God, my God, why have you forsaken me?" Having thus established him in solidarity with us sinners, God

"did not spare his own Son but gave him up for us all"....

The Eucharist is the greatest gift of himself

610 Jesus gave the supreme expression of his free offering of himself at the meal shared with the twelve Apostles "on the night he was betrayed."....

In the Eucharist, Jesus consecrated new priests

611 The Eucharist that Christ institutes at that moment will be the memorial of his sacrifice. Jesus includes the apostles in his own offering and bids them perpetuate it. By doing so, the Lord institutes his apostles as priests of the New Covenant....

Jesus' sacrifice is the highest of all

614 This sacrifice of Christ is unique; it completes and surpasses all other sacrifices....

Jesus' sacrifice surpasses yet embraces everyone

616 ...The existence in Christ of the divine person of the Son, who at once surpasses and embraces all human persons and constitutes himself as the Head of all mankind, makes possible his redemptive sacrifice *for all*.

We look to the cross for our hope

617 The Council of Trent emphasizes the unique character of Christ's sacrifice as "the source of eternal salvation"...and teaches that "his most holy Passion on the wood of the cross merited justification for us."....

All, especially Mary, must share his redemptive suffering

618 ...He calls his disciples to "take up [their] cross and follow [him]"...for Christ also suffered for [us], leaving [us] an example so that [we] should follow in his steps."...In fact Jesus desires to associate with his redeeming sacrifice those who were to be its

first beneficiaries....This is achieved supremely in
the case of his mother....

The empty tomb attests to the resurrection

640 ...The first element we encounter in the
framework of the Easter events is the empty tomb.
In itself it is not a direct proof of Resurrection....
Nonetheless the empty tomb was still an essential
sign for all. Its discovery by the disciples was the
first step toward recognizing the very fact of the
Resurrection....

The resurrection was predicted in the Old Testament

652 Christ's Resurrection is the fulfillment of the
promises both of the Old Testament and of Jesus
himself during his earthly life....

In the divine Jesus is God's promise fulfilled

653 The truth of Jesus' divinity is confirmed by his
Resurrection. He had said: "When you have lifted
up the Son of man, then you will know that I am
he."....

We are set free as well as adopted

654 The Paschal mystery has two aspects: by his
death, Christ liberates us from sin; by his
Resurrection, he opens for us the way to a new
life....

His resurrection anticipates our own

655 Finally, Christ's Resurrection—and the risen
Christ himself—is the principle and source of our
future resurrection....

The ascension closes Jesus' post-resurrection appearances

659 ...Jesus' final apparition ends with the
irreversible entry of his humanity into divine glory,
symbolized by the cloud and by heaven, where he
is seated from that time forward at God's right
hand....Only in a wholly exceptional and unique

way would Jesus show himself to Paul "as to one untimely born," in a last apparition that established him as an apostle....

We live in the end times

670 ...We are already at "the last hour."....

God will triumph over evil

677 ...The kingdom will be fulfilled, then, not by a historic triumph of the Church through a progressive ascendancy, but only by God's victory over the final unleashing of evil, which will cause his Bride to come down from heaven....God's triumph over the revolt of evil will take the form of the Last Judgment after the final cosmic upheaval of this passing world....

In the presentation of Jesus Christ, eternal Son of God, in the *Catechism of the Catholic Church*, we discover a portrait of one who gave all people filial adoption by becoming part of our fallen humanity. He was born into the house of Israel from a Jewish woman and lived according to the Law. His person reveals the life of the Trinity and his dependence on his eternal relationship with the Father.

At 12 years of age, even in the presence of Joseph, he confirms his birth from the virgin, born of God. In his public life he is recognized by his disciples and by people as being the Messiah of Israel. He is the divine "I Am" who came down from Heaven for us and for our salvation, becoming the suffering servant and dying on the cross to reconcile the human race with the Father in the divine plan of filial adoption.

By offering himself in sacrifice in the Eucharist, he sealed the eternal covenant, manifesting the universality of salvation and of sin. This universal redemption, fulfilled on the cross, manifested its power of salvation in the resurrection of Christ, the Lord, who is now exalted on the right hand of the Father, ready to send the Spirit to the humanity he reconciled with God.

God the Son in Liturgical Tradition

As in the previous chapter on God the Father, so too do we look to liturgical prayer for a summary of God the Son, Jesus Christ. This summary can be found in various Roman Rite liturgical texts and the Maronite Hoosoyo or Prayer of Forgiveness of Pentecost:

Roman Rite	**Maronite Rite**
In glory at the right hand of God, you gave the Gift of the Father to your disciples, send forth your Spirit to renew the world (Liturgy of the Hours, Intercessions, Morning Prayer, Pentecost).	May we be worthy to praise, confess and glorify the Sun of Justice who has shown his resplendent glory in the upper room. He confirmed the minds of the twelve apostles. He harmoniously divided the tongues over the simple, fulfilling each one. He breathed into them the understanding of the Spirit, the Paraclete, and granted them his wisdom. He commanded them to go out to the four corners of the earth, announce to the nations the true faith and convert the world from error. To him are due glory and honor, now and for ever. Amen.
	On this day, the apostles tasted of the divine wine of the grace flowing from the life-giving Spirit; on that account, the Jews thought they were drunk from ordinary wine.

Roman Rite

Christ the Lord has gathered his Church in unity through the Spirit. With sure hope let us ask him: *Lord, make the whole world new.*

Lord Jesus, when you were raised high upon the cross, streams of living water flowed from your pierced side, pour out on us your life-giving Spirit. In glory at the right hand of God, you gave the Gift of the Father to your disciples, send forth your Spirit to renew the world (Liturgy of the Hours, Intercessions, Morning Prayer, Pentecost).

Maronite Rite

O Christ our God, glorious light, as you enlighten minds, the heavenly powers in beauty extol you, your Father and your Holy Spirit. For our sake, you willed to descend and mingle with us. You accepted to be born of the flesh from the blessed Virgin. You achieved that by which you saved us: your birth, crucifixion, death and resurrection. When you chose to ascend to the Father, you gathered your apostles in the upper room. By the laying of your hands, you blessed them and anointed them through the grace of your priesthood. You breathed in them the Holy Spirit and told them, "Stay in Jerusalem until I send you the Paraclete from the Father. He will teach you and bestow upon you his wisdom with abundance. For, as long as I stay with you, the Paraclete will not be sent to you." With these words, you confirmed your holy disciples, then ascended to heaven accompanied by the joyous shouts of the angels. You sit on the throne of glory at the right hand of your Father. Then, on this holy day of Pentecost, you dwelt within them in the gentleness of the Holy Spirit, established in them your divine gifts, wisdom and knowledge. You taught them the tongues of all nations of the earth.

Roman Rite

Maronite Rite

On this day, Simon Peter, Andrew, the sons of Zebedee and the other apostles stood in joy and exultation, for they witnessed the fulfillment of the promise the Son made to them.

Today we celebrate the great beginning of your Church when the Holy Spirit made known to all peoples the one true God, and created from the many languages of man one voice to profess one faith (Eucharistic Prayer, Pentecost).

On this day of the coming of the Paraclete, the upper room in Jerusalem became the new Babel; but now, by the power of the Spirit, people were instructed by the apostles in the grace of the true good news.

On this day, Judas the Iscariot stood in astonishment as he saw the apostles clothed in glorious light and illuminating their weaknesses with divine mysteries.

Through the Spirit you make all things new, heal the sick, comfort the distressed, give salvation to all. Through the Spirit you raised your Son from the dead, raise up the bodies of the dead into everlasting life (Liturgy of the Hours, Intercessions, Evening Prayer II, Pentecost).

Therefore, we petition your unspeakable love for all people to pour upon us the grace of your life-giving Spirit. Purify us from the thorns of sin. Make us worthy to offer you spiritual fruits of virtue, faith, love and true hope. Establish your peace in your holy Church. In your mercy, visit the sick, the needy and those who solicit our humble prayers. In your loving humanity, remember kindly our parents, brothers and sisters, teachers and all the

Roman Rite	Maronite Rite
	faithful departed so that, together, we may be worthy of the reward promised by you, your Father and your Holy Spirit, now and for ever. Amen (Hoosoyo, Prayer of Forgiveness, addressed to the Son, Feast of Pentecost).

Let us look at some of the details of the prayer summarizing the life of the Son.

The Incarnation

The coming of Jesus heralds a new day

Roman Rite	Maronite Rite
Christ is your Son before all ages, yet now he is born in time. He has come to lift up all things to himself, to restore unity to creation, and to lead mankind from exile into your heavenly kingdom. With all the angels of heaven we sing our joyful hymn of praise... (Eucharistic Prayer, Christmas II).	On this day, the angels left their dwellings to honor the Son. On this day, the stable rejoices, the manger exalts, and Bethlehem is filled with glory. On this day, the prophets stir in their tombs, for the dawn of a new age has appeared. Today, the Lord Jesus is born of the blessed Virgin Mary, and he has liberated all people from their captors. Let us raise a hymn of glory to the Father, Son and Holy Spirit, now and for ever. Amen.

Roman Rite

O sacred Lord of ancient Israel, who showed yourself to Moses in the burning bush, who gave him the holy law on Sinai mountain: come, stretch out your mighty hand to set us free (Liturgy of the Hours, Canticle of Mary, Evening Prayer, December 18).

Almighty God and Father of light, a child is born for us and a son is given to us. Your eternal Word leaped down from heaven in the silent watches of the night, and now your Church is filled with wonder at the nearness of her God.

Open our hearts to receive his life and increase our vision with the rising of dawn, that our lives may be filled with his glory and his peace, who lives and reigns for ever and ever (Liturgy of the Hours, Alternative Prayer, Morning Prayer, Christmas).

Maronite Rite

The righteous and just desired to witness this day. Through the ages, they predicted in prophecy your blessed coming. When you created Adam, he saw your mystery, and he yearned to be a god. Moses depicted your birth in a burning bush which was not consumed, yet you dwelt in the Virgin Mary, and she was not harmed by your flame. King David spoke of the virgin birth, and Jeremiah called you "Root of Jesse." "Shoot of David." Each of these prepared for your birth through their visions and words.

Holy Lord, Hidden Being, you became visible at Bethlehem. Holy Lord, Fair Dawn, you enlightened the whole world.

Holy Lord, Wisdom of the Father, you became a child to free the children of Adam.

Holy Lord, Bread of Life, you came to earth to feed us.

Holy Lord, Mighty God, you accepted mortality to show your love for us.

Roman Rite

Good shepherd of God's flock, gather all into your Church. Lord Jesus, help the shepherds of your pilgrim people, until you come again may they zealously feed your flock. Choose from among us heralds of your word, to proclaim your Gospel to the ends of the earth. Take pity on all who struggle and fall along the way, may they find a friend to help them. Show your glory in heaven, to those who listen to your voice on earth (Liturgy of the Hours, Intercessions, Evening Prayer, Friday of the First Week of Advent).

Maronite Rite

Your flock sings "Holy" to you and petitions you to keep all harm and scandal far from it. Guard the living and forgive the dead. Heal the sick and restore the failing. Watch over the priests and clothe our leaders with integrity. Teach youth moderation. Instruct the elderly in wisdom and patience. Make us all worthy to celebrate your holy incarnation. Glory to you, Father, Son and Holy Spirit, and may mercy be upon us, now and for ever. Amen (Hoosoyo, Prayer of Forgiveness, Feast of the Birth of the Lord).

The Circumcision

The sign of Jesus' circumcision is fulfilled by baptism

Roman Rite

Maronite Rite

May we be worthy to praise, confess and glorify the One Who fulfilled the prophets by His amazing incarnation and perfected the symbols of the past by His wondrous birth. He concluded the law of Moses when He appeared, and he completed the Mysteries of Abraham when he was circumcised. When he

Roman Rite	Maronite Rite
	became man, he put an end to all parables and prophecies. To the Good One are due glory and honor, now and for ever. Amen.

Glory to you, Christ our God, only Word of the Father, You willed to free us from agony of sin. You were born as God-Incarnate from the Virgin's womb that we might be born again by the Spirit of life. After your birth, your divine nature remained unchanged, and you were like us in all things but sin. Eight days after your birth, you were circumcised to fulfill the patterns the prophets had foretold. From Abraham, circumcision had been the sign of your people. Now in its place, you have established holy baptism. You made faith the sign and seal of your covenant with us, and you circumcised our hearts with a new spirit of adoption. You gathered a new people, a redeemed Israel, reconciled now by our faith to you.

O Lord, as you renewed sinful man, now renew your Church. Remove the scandal of those who reject your humanity and deny your divinity. Purify us that we may rejoice with all the children |

Roman Rite	Maronite Rite
	of your covenant, now and for ever. Amen (Hoosoyo, Prayer of Forgiveness, Feast of the Circumcision of the Lord).

The Finding in the Temple

Roman Rite	Maronite Rite
	May we be worthy to glorify the Father who sent his Son for our salvation and to praise the Son whom the prophets and men of old longed to see. He came to explain the ways of his Father to the scribes and pharisees in the temple. May we honor the living Spirit who spoke through prophets and apostles. Glory and honor are due to the good One on this feast and all the days of our lives, now and for ever. Amen.
	Blessed are you, our Lord and God, Jesus Christ. You accepted our human nature in order to sanctify us and to raise us to yourself. With Mary and Joseph, you obediently went to the temple at Jerusalem to fulfill the law which you had put in the hands of the prophets in times past. On this day, instruct us also, divine Teacher, that we may belong to

Roman Rite	Maronite Rite

the household of God as members of his living temple, for our lives have no meaning except in God.

Gracious Lord, we now ask you to turn the light of your gaze upon our thoughts. Let us know of your love for us which is at the source and foundation of all your commands. Guide us, that we may joyfully embrace your sacred counsels. Protect and inspire those who shepherd your Church and enlighten us, so we may understand their apostolic teachings. Uproot from your Church every heresy and tendency which leads to destruction, so that your gospel may become a beacon of light and a harbor of safety. Let our hearts know true happiness, that we may enjoy your living, Holy Spirit, now and for ever. Amen (Hoosoyo, Prayer of Forgiveness, Feast of the Finding of Jesus in the Temple).

Epiphany and Baptism

The Fountain of Holiness is baptized in the river

Roman Rite	Maronite Rite
You celebrated your new gift of baptism by signs and wonders at the Jordan. Your voice was heard from heaven to awaken faith in the presence among us of the Word made man. Your Spirit was seen as a dove, revealing Jesus as your servant, and anointing him with joy as the Christ, sent to bring to the poor the good news of salvation (Preface, Baptism of the Lord). Three mysteries mark this holy day: today the star leads the Magi to the infant Christ; today water is changed into wine for the wedding feast; today Christ wills to be baptized by John in the river Jordan to bring us salvation (Liturgy of the Hours, Canticle of Mary, Evening Prayer II, Epiphany).	May we be worthy to praise, glorify and honor the hidden Father who thundered from the heavens and acknowledged his only beloved; the adored Son who was revealed at the river and baptized by his servant; the Holy Spirit who was seen in heaven and on earth and made known his coming. The Father spoke to creation through his beloved Son and declared his truth. The Creator Son was baptized in the river and instructed us in the form of a dove and revealed him to us. Glory and thanksgiving are due to him, now and for ever. Amen. Almighty God and Savior Jesus Christ: you are the merciful One. You inclined your everlasting mercy to give salvation to our weak and feeble race. For our sake, you became man of the holy Virgin Mary. From the Magi and shepherds, you received mystical and royal gifts. You grew in wisdom and perfection. And though you were the fountain of holiness, you were baptized in

Roman Rite

Almighty, eternal God, when the Spirit descended upon Jesus at his baptism in the Jordan, you revealed him as your own beloved Son. Keep us, your children born of water and the Spirit, faithful to our calling (Opening Prayer, Feast of the Baptism of the Lord).

Maronite Rite

the Jordan River by your forerunner, John, so that by your baptism, water would be made holy to bring us to a new birth.

Therefore, O Christ our God, we beseech and implore you through this incense which we offer on this festive and holy day. We intercede with you, O Christ Lord, for you are the great abyss filled with unspeakable mysteries, and you have enlightened all creation with the bright and blessed rays of your divinity. You are God who was seen in the flesh, and we, of the flesh, were transformed by the gifts of the Spirit. O Lord, we ask and implore you, grant pardon of debts and forgiveness of sins to all your flock on this day of your Epiphany. You are God who was seen at the Jordan River through the unspeakable mysteries of your Holy Trinity, One in essence. From the heights, the Father declared and said to us: "This is my beloved Son." O God the Word, You are one of the Trinity who, by your holy baptism, has shown us the light of your Trinity. We beseech and ask you, O God of the soul, be pleased with us on this feast day and accept these petitions and adoration from your flock which we offer you with the fragrance of this

Roman Rite	Maronite Rite
	incense. Comfort us with the protection and fullness of your holy, life-giving commandments.
Lord, let the light of your glory shine within us, and lead us through the darkness of this world to the radiant joy of our eternal home (Liturgy of the Hours, Prayer, Evening Prayer, Monday after Epiphany to Baptism).	May our lives, actions and undertakings be to the glory of your love for all people and for the absolution and salvation of our souls. May we be led to the paradise of light with your righteous. May we be worthy to hear the voice that says: "Come, blessed of my Father. Inherit the kingdom prepared for you before the foundation of the world." We ask this through the intercession of all the saints, now and for ever. Amen (Hoosoyo, Prayer of Forgiveness, Feast of Epiphany).

Jesus' Public Life

In the Roman Rite, the weeks before Easter are filled with references to the things Jesus did during his ministry among the people, sometimes healing miracles, sometimes not. It is interesting for the theme of this book that his transfiguration is the focus of the eucharistic prayer for the second Sunday in Lent. In the Maronite Rite, which has no changing cycle of readings as in the Roman Rite, seven events in the life of Jesus—each displaying a miracle (mostly of healing)—are celebrated each of the seven Sundays. Cana Sunday introduces the great season of Lent:

Roman Rite	Maronite Rite
	May we be worthy to praise, confess and glorify the Bridegroom who betrothed the Church with his blood and sanctified himself for her; the merciful Son of Man who, on a day like today, joined in the celebration of the sons of men; the good One to whom glory and honor on this feast and all the days of our lives, now and for ever. Amen.

Glory to you, O lofty One. You descended from your Father to visit the sons of men and look after them in your mercy. On a day like this, you changed water to wine as a sign of us. The crowd saw your greatness, and the disciples believed in you.

Now we petition you, O generous and good God, let us drink from the new wine. We will drink of your love and rejoice at your wedding feast. May your eternal light enlighten a world in search of true joy and living water. May it come to know the pure Fountain and drink from it. May your blessing descend upon Christian families and upon those who have vowed to be faithful to married life. May they walk

Roman Rite	Maronite Rite
	according to your laws and live their lives according to their faith in you. To you are due glory and honor, now and for ever. Amen (Hoosoyo, Prayer of Forgiveness, Cana Sunday).

On the Sunday of the Healing of the Leper, we find the following prayer:

Roman Rite	Maronite Rite
	May we be worthy to praise, confess and glorify the merciful Father who created us in his love. He had compassion on us and sent his only Son who renewed our nature and vivified us with his own life. He sent his Holy Spirit, without whom there is no holiness. Let us confess the good One to whom are due glory and thanksgiving on this feast and all the days of our lives, now and for ever. Amen.
	O Christ our God, Physician of souls and bodies, to you we raise our eyes and hearts, imploring you never to keep your mercy and grace from us. But look upon us and have compassion, as you had compassion on the leper. Come to us, cleanse us and make us

Roman Rite

Maronite Rite

whole. You have said: "Ask, and it will be given, knock, and it will be opened."

Therefore, with unfailing hope, we implore you, Lord of salvation: out of your love for us, forgive our sins; because of your grace, heal us; accept those who repent; bring back the wandering. Come and console the sorrowful and strengthen the weak. Feed the hungry and help the poor. Bless the rich and enrich them with good deeds. Remember the faithful departed who sleep in hope of you. For we glorify you, Father, Son and Holy Spirit, now and for ever. Amen (Hoosoyo, Prayer of Forgiveness, Sunday of the Leper).

On the Sunday of the Healing of the Hemorrhaging Woman, the Prayer of Forgiveness is particularly tender:

Roman Rite

Maronite Rite

May we be worthy to praise, confess and glorify the Father who had compassion on us and sent his only begotten Son to save us. Let us confess the Son who bound our wounds and poured his healing ointment upon them.

Roman Rite	Maronite Rite
	We thank the living Holy Spirit who strengthens those who come to him. Honor and glory are due to the good one, now and for ever. Amen.

We give thanks, O Lord, for who
you are and for what you have
done for us. We ask you to stretch
forth your powerful right arm to
us and rest your loving gaze upon
us. Let us not be tempted by the
world and by what is in it. Let us
not forget that we were created
for you and that our hearts are
yours alone. We know that
sickness and disease are spread
throughout our souls and that
strong and destructive winds are
blowing through our thoughts

Roman Rite	Maronite Rite

and minds. Be not far from us, O Lord, when times grow dark and threatening. Do not let despair dominate us. Heal us, O God, as you healed the paralytic and the blind man, the hemorrhaging woman and the lame. Spread your peace throughout our souls, as you spread peace over the surging waves and calmed them.

We implore you, O Lord, for all the suffering, for those in need and for those who are overcome with sorrow. Pour the balm of your consolation on their wounded hearts. May the gaze of your face be their healing medicine and your fatherly eye keep watch over them, lest they stray from your love when sorrow and misfortune wound their hearts. Raise your right hand and bless us all, so true joy may reign within us. And we will praise and extol the glorious Trinity, now and for ever. Amen (Hoosoyo, Prayer of Forgiveness, Sunday of the Hemorrhaging Woman).

Inserted into the seven Maronite Lenten Sundays recalling God's healing mercy is the story of the prodigal son:

Roman Rite	Maronite Rite

Maronite Rite

May we be worthy to praise,
glorify and honor the merciful
Father who loves us and accepts
our repentance. His Son became
man and taught love to our race,
and his Holy Spirit enlightened
our minds and hearts. Glory and
honor to the good One on this
day and for ever. Amen.

O Christ our God, you are true
Light come into the world. You
are the way which leads to the
Father. You counseled us with
penance, mercy and living water.
Today, it is your will that we recall
the parable of the prodigal son
who turned from his error, put
faith in his father and wept for sin.

O Lord, during this season of
lent, send your Spirit to sinners,
so that, in seeking forgiveness,
they may return to you. Open
your loving arms to them and
prepare a crown for them, so that,
cheerfully, they may meet you
and know your comfort.

Make us who petition you,
apostles, who proclaim your
gospel by our lives and actions.
We will announce your word to all
people, our brothers and sisters,
sons and daughters of the

Roman Rite	Maronite Rite
	heavenly Father, all redeemed by your pure blood. And may your Spirit be our strength and help, that we may praise you throughout our lives, now and for ever. Amen (Hoosoyo, Prayer of Forgiveness, Sunday of the Prodigal Son).

On the Sunday of the Paralytic, the prayer theme continues to display the Lord's healing mercy:

Roman Rite	Maronite Rite
	May we be worthy to glorify, praise and honor the Father who made us sharers in his divine life. The Son came into the world to heal suffering humanity, and the Holy Spirit poured out his consolation upon our broken hearts. Glory and honor are due to the good One, now and for ever. Amen.

O Christ, Word of the Father and only Son, you partook of our lives, so we might partake of yours. You encouraged the paralytic to pick up his stretcher and walk, so that the crowds would profess your divinity. You have brought joy to the suffering and light to the blind. You put |

Roman Rite	Maronite Rite
	new hope in the heart of the bereaved widow. Increase our faith in you, O Christ, Son of the living God. Confirm us in hope and let your pure blood be for the forgiveness of our sins. O Lord, we thank you for the generous gift you have given your church: in your name, sins are absolved, and the repentant are healed, in your name, the weak of faith are strengthened, and the hesitant are encouraged. Blessed are you at all times with your Father and Holy Spirit, for ever. Amen (Hoosoyo, Prayer of Forgiveness, Sunday of the Paralytic).

Closing the seven Sundays recalling the miraculous ministry of Jesus is the Sunday of the Healing of the Blind Man:

Roman Rite	Maronite Rite
	May we be worthy to glorify, praise and honor the true and only Spirit: The Father is the source of eternal Light; the Son is Light From Light; the Holy Spirit proceeds from the Father and Son—One God, forever praised. Glory and honor to the good One

Roman Rite	Maronite Rite
	on this feast and all the days of our lives, for ever.

O Christ our God, your light filled the world, but the people were fond of darkness. We are your people, sons and daughters of light, who believe and hope in you as their true Light. Heal our wounds and soothe our pain. Wipe away our sinfulness and fill us with your peace and tranquility.

Grant us your love, preserve your Church and keep her as a shining light in the world. Protect her children until the end of time and gather them into the unity of the Holy Spirit. Rid them of hatred and revenge and bring them home to your eternal Light. There, with all your people, they will glorify you, Father, Son and Holy Spirit, for ever. Amen (Hoosoyo, Prayer of Forgiveness, Sunday of the Paralytic).

The Triumphal Entry into Jerusalem

Hosanna Sunday—Passion (Palm) Sunday in the Roman Rite—recalls Jesus' triumphal entry into Jerusalem:

Roman Rite	**Maronite Rite**
The days of his life-giving death and glorious resurrection are approaching. This is the hour when he triumphed over Satan's pride, the time when we celebrate the great event of our redemption.	May we be worthy to praise, glorify and thank the King of kings who is exalted on high. He is seated on a lofty throne while the seraphim praise him with: "Holy, Holy, Holy," and cherubim acclaim him with: "Blessed is the Lord, and wonderful is his name." He has chosen to ride on a lowly animal to enter Jerusalem to the accompaniment of the shouts of children. Glory and honor to him on this day and all the days of our lives, for ever. Amen.
Through Christ the angels of heaven offer their prayer of adoration as they rejoice in your presence for ever. May our voices be one with theirs in their triumphant hymn of praise:	
Holy, holy, holy Lord, God of power and might, heaven and earth are full of your glory. Hosanna in the highest. Blessed is he who comes in the name of the Lord. Hosanna in the highest (Eucharistic Prayer II, Passion of the Lord).	
God grant that with the angels and the children we may be faithful, and sing with them to the conqueror of death: Hosanna in the highest (Liturgy of the Hours, Antiphon 2, Morning Prayer, Passion Sunday).	Rejoice today, O David, and exalt, O Zechariah. Be glad, O Moses, and all you prophets be joyful. All of your prophecies are fulfilled, and your sayings are accomplished this day in Christ. For the King of Sion, mounted on

144

Roman Rite

The great crowd that had gathered for the feast cried out to the Lord: Blessed is he who comes in the name of the Lord. Hosanna in the highest (Liturgy of the Hours, Antiphon 1, Morning Prayer, Passion Sunday).

Look with love on those who suffer because of our indifference, come to their aid, and turn our uncaring hearts to works of justice and charity...Transform the bodies of the dead to be like your own in glory, and bring us at last into their fellowship (Liturgy of

Maronite Rite

a lowly colt, enters his city amid praises of children. His apostles and followers shout: "Blessed is he who comes in the name of the Lord! Blessed the King of Israel!"

Blessed are the mouths that praised God's Son and more blessed yet are the hands that waved olive branches to welcome the King. Blessed are those who sang and cheered for the most High of Israel. To their number, the Church joins all her generations of children from the nations of the earth. In her churches and monasteries, they gather to go out to meet their Lord. Young and old carry branches and candles. Lights and banners announce their celebration as they sing their songs of praise and say: "Blessed is he who comes in the name of the Lord! Blessed is Christ our King!"

And today, O Christ our King, your Church raises her voice in prayer to you. Grant wisdom to her leaders, that they may teach and guide. Strengthen her children in true faith, that they may fearlessly confess you. Confirm her monks and nuns in

Roman Rite	**Maronite Rite**
the Hours, Intercessions, Evening Prayer II, Passion Sunday).	the ways of perfection. Aid the weak and guide the faltering. Comfort the sick and visit the aged. Prepare a place for our departed in your heavenly kingdom, and all its churches will offer you praise and honor for ever. Amen (Hoosoyo, Prayer of Forgiveness, Hosanna Sunday).

The Death of Jesus

Jesus becomes a servant

Roman Rite	**Maronite Rite**

Father,
by the power of the Holy Spirit,
you anointed your only Son
  Messiah and Lord of creation;
you have given us a share in his
  consecration
to priestly service in your Church.
Help us to be faithful witnesses in
  the world
to the salvation Christ won for all
  mankind
(Opening Prayer, Chrism Mass of
Holy Thursday).
	May we be worthy to praise, glorify and honor the most High and exalted One who willed to humble himself and accept death. He bore our human condition out of compassion and accomplished his plan of salvation out of loving kindness. In humility, he washed his disciples' feet and taught them the great and hidden mystery of his descent to our weakness. In so doing, he imparted an authentic example to be handed down to his Church. Glory and honor to him, now and for ever. Amen.

Roman Rite

May the Morning Star which
   never sets find this flame still
   burning:
      Christ, that Morning Star,
      who came back from the
      dead,
      and shed his peaceful light
      on all mankind,
      your Son who lives and
      reigns for ever and ever
(Easter Proclamation, Easter
Vigil).

Almighty, ever-living God,
you have given the human race
   Jesus Christ our Savior
as a model of humility.
He fulfilled your will
by becoming man and giving his
   life on the cross.
Help us to bear witness to you
by following his example of
   suffering
and make us worthy to share in
   his resurrection
(Opening Prayer, Passion Sunday).

Maronite Rite

O Lord Jesus Christ, God the
Word, you are the Lord of heaven
and earth and the consuming
Flame upon whom the fiery ranks
of heaven dare not look. In your
compassion, you clothed yourself
with a body. The heavenly
creatures who serve you with
reverence hide their faces before
you.

Almighty God, source of life, in
your mercy, you chose to bow your
head before the creation of your
hands. You washed your disciples'
feet and imparted an authentic
example of your humility for us to
follow. You have shown us how to
imitate your saving meekness. Now,
allow us, your servants gathered
here before you, to cleanse
ourselves from every trace of sin as
we follow the example of your
humility. May our minds be
illuminated by the way you
humbled yourself. Through your
humility, may we loose the bonds of
vanity and the destructive
tendencies of the adversary. May
we put on humility, gladness and
true love, for you instructed us to
serve each other with the purity
and holiness worthy of true
disciples and servants. May we

Roman Rite	Maronite Rite
(See previous page for parallel text.)	preserve the memory of your saving passion and your life-giving death, so we may observe the feast of your glorious resurrection. And we will glorify you, now and for ever. Amen (Hoosoyo, Prayer of Forgiveness, Thursday of the Mysteries [Holy Thursday]).

Jesus dies on the cross

Roman Rite	Maronite Rite
For our sake he opened his arms on the cross; he put an end to death and revealed the resurrection. In this he fulfilled your will and won for you a holy people (Eucharistic Prayer, Weekdays VI).	May we be worthy to praise, glorify and honor the heavenly Peacemaker who was hung on a cross. He opened his arms and gathered all people. The Lord became incarnate, ascended to the far regions of his cross and received glory and authentic worship from the ends of the earth. The good Shepherd showed his love to his flock by caring for his sheep. He saved all people by his cross and forgave the sins of all men by his sacrifice. Glory and honor to the good One, now and for ever. Amen.
Blessed be God, the giver of salvation, who decreed that mankind should become a new	We worship and confess your divinity, O God, for you created us in your image and formed us

Roman Rite

creation in himself, when all
would be made new. With great
confidence, let us ask him: Lord,
renew us in your Spirit (Liturgy of
the Hours, Intercessions,
Morning Prayer, Wednesday of
the Fifth Week of Lent).

When your children sinned
and wandered far from your
    friendship,
you reunited them with yourself
through the blood of your Son
and the power of the Holy Spirit
(Eucharistic Prayer, Sundays in
Ordinary Time VIII).

Lord Jesus, when your side was
pierced, there flowed out blood
and water, the marvelous symbol
of the whole Church, through
your death, burial and
resurrection, bring life to your
bride the Church (Liturgy of the
Hours, Intercessions, Evening
Prayer, Holy Saturday).

Lifted high on the cross,
Christ gave his life for us,
so much did he love us.
From his wounded side flowed
    blood and water,
the fountain of sacramental life in

Maronite Rite

in your likeness. We praise your
salvation, O Lover of all. On this
Friday, you gave us life by your
cross and set us free by your
death. In the beginning, you
completed our creation on the
sixth day. Your hands formed
mortal man from the dust of the
earth, and you modeled and
created him in your image. From
your own mouth, you breathed
the breath of life into him. Thus,
he was fashioned in beauty and
perfected in knowledge—a
marvelous creation! But in his
innocence, man wandered,
neglected your command and was
delivered to judgment. Death now
entered to distort your creation.

But even after this, O
compassionate and loving Lord,
your mercy prevailed. On the
sixth day, another Friday filled
with mysteries, your hands were
pierced with nails on the cross. At
the hands of your executioners,
you were humiliated, and your
side was pierced to give people
life. New life flowed with the
blood and water from your side,
and you won the people back and
renewed them.

Roman Rite	Maronite Rite
the Church. To his open heart the Savior invites all men, to draw water in joy from the springs of salvation (Eucharistic Prayer, Masses of the Sacred Heart).	*(See previous page for parallel text.)*

Father of mercy, hear the prayers of your repentant children who call on you in love. Enlighten our minds and sanctify our hearts (Liturgy of the Hours, Prayer, Evening Prayer, Wednesday of the Fifth Week of Lent).	Again today, on this Friday of your saving passion and the memorial of your life-giving cross, the Church petitions you through the mouths of her children with the fragrance of this incense. As in the beginning, you created out of love and then returned to save and give life, visit once again your creation and grant peace to the whole world by your cross.

By the merits of your Son's death, hear us, Lord.	By your cross, remove anger and put an end to war. By your cross, eliminate strife and retribution. By your cross, calm disorders and pacify the angry. By your cross, humble the proud, expose the self-serving and remove the enemy. By your cross, curb violence and anger. Establish your Church in strength and make her monasteries firm. By your cross, let the priests be honorable and the deacons reverent.
Give unity to your Church. Protect N., our Pope. Increase faith and understanding in those under instruction. Gather all Christians in unity. Lead the Jewish people to the fullness of redemption. Enlighten with your glory those who do not yet believe in Christ. Show the marks of your love in creation to those who deny them. Guide the minds and hearts of all who are troubled.	

Roman Rite

Have pity on those who have died
(Liturgy of the Hours,
Intercessions, Evening Prayer,
Good Friday).

Lord,
send down your abundant
    blessing
upon your people who have
    devoutly recalled the death of
    your Son
in the sure hope of the
    resurrection.
Grant them pardon; bring them
    comfort.
May their faith grow stronger
and their eternal salvation be
    assured
(Prayer over the People, Good
Friday).

Maronite Rite

Sustain the elderly, subdue the
haste of youth and rear the young.
By your cross, pardon sinners,
forgive wrongdoers and guard
your flock which now worships
before you. For your Church
glorifies you in the sign of the
cross.

Save us and all your people.
Completely perfect us in your
strength. Visit us and revive us, so
that our image may be renewed
and our likeness recovered. May
we emerge from this mournful
vigil with every tear wiped away in
the hope of your consolation.
Then we shall wear your glory
and put on your light. Make us
worthy to meet the day of your
resurrection as heirs in the
kingdom. Then without ceasing,
we shall glorify you, for ever.
Amen (Hoosoyo, Prayer of
Forgiveness, Great Friday [Good
Friday]).

The Resurrection

*The glory Jesus received at the transfiguration
now shines resplendently upon him*

Roman Rite	Maronite Rite

Roman Rite

Through your resurrection you became our peace and reconciliation, unite the baptized in perfect communion of faith and love (Liturgy of the Hours, Intercessions, Evening Prayer, Thursday of the Fourth Week of Easter).

Maronite Rite

May we be worthy to praise, confess and glorify true peace and the God and Lord of all peace. You have saved the world from the scourge of sin and reconciled our weak nature to your Father and Holy Spirit. May your peace now reign among us and dwell within us. May it guide our steps, that we may avoid all hatred and dishonesty. May we remain in peace with each other, leave this world in peace and inherit that peace promised to all peacemakers. Then we shall offer you praise and thanksgiving without end, Father, Son and Holy Spirit, now and for ever. Amen.

O God, you are true Love and the source of all love and peace. In your divine mercy, you promised peace to your disciples when you said, "Peace I give you, my peace I leave with you." O Lord, make us worthy of this peace, now and always.

Roman Rite

Maronite Rite

Your peace rescued Noah from the flood and sent him a dove with an olive branch of peace. Your peace opened a way through the sea for the Hebrews and strengthened their steps through the water. With the angel Gabriel, you sent a greeting of peace to the Virgin Mary and promised peace to sinful Adam after he was tempted. You sent a greeting of peace to the shepherds and showed them the Peace who would reign over the world. You calmed the raging sea when the disciples' boat was faltering, and your peace removed fear from their hearts. You gave your disciples peace when you said, "Peace I give to you. May my peace which is not of this world reign around you."

Be our great joy that no one can take from us, so that we may reject sin with its sadness, and reach out to eternal life (Liturgy of the Hours, Intercessions, Morning Prayer, Saturday of the Second Week of Easter).

Now O Lord, establish peace in your Church and drive away from her division and conflict. Keep the promises which you made to her and save her from the jaws of death. Unite her children and adorn them with love. Stir up in them true charity for one another and strengthen them in the faith. Let them radiate with holy conduct, clothe them with humility and fill them with joy. Purify them from the spirit of

Roman Rite

Maronite Rite

malice and anger and liberate them from deceit and hypocrisy. Extinguish all causes of division and conflict, so that, adorned with virtue and liberated from vice, they may be worthy to dwell in your holy temple. May they be worthy to join your heavenly gathering and eternally share in the joy of this festival, now and for ever. Amen (Hoosoyo, Prayer of Forgiveness, Sunday of the Resurrection of the Lord).

Lord, you walked the way of suffering and crucifixion, may we suffer and die with you, and rise again to share your glory.

Son of the Father, our master and brother, you have made us a kingdom of priests for our God, may we offer you our joyful sacrifice of praise.

King of glory, we look forward to the great day of your coming in splendor, that we may see you face to face, and be transformed in your likeness (Liturgy of the Hours, Intercessions, Morning Prayer, Third Sunday of Easter).

O Lord Jesus Christ, by your living cross, you have saved us from going astray and have given us a way to heaven. By your cross, worshipers are kept safe, and Christians are protected. By your cross, may children be reared and may men and women live lives of purity. By the sign of your cross, may the aged be made wise, the sick be restored to health, the priests holy and the deacons reverent. May the Church flourish with her monks and nuns. May peace and harmony reign among your people. For your cross will guard us from all distress and will lead us to perfection. In purity and holiness, we renew this memorial of your resurrection. And at your second coming, O Lord, make us worthy to meet you

Roman Rite	Maronite Rite
	in joy. We will praise you, O, Father, Son and Holy Spirit, now and for ever. Amen (Prayer of the Rite of Peace, Sunday of the Resurrection of the Lord).

The Ascension

Jesus' work done on earth, he goes home to heaven

Roman Rite	Maronite Rite
God ascends to shouts of joy, alleluia, alleluia. The Lord to the blast of trumpets, alleluia, alleluia (Liturgy of the Hours, Responsory, Evening Prayer I, Ascension).	May we be worthy to praise, glorify and honor the true Word of God. He came down from heaven for our salvation and clothed himself with flesh from the Blessed Virgin Mary. He suffered, died for us and arose on the third day. He ascended today in glory amid blasts of trumpets and triumph, to bring back to his Father's house those gone astray. To the good One is due glory and honor on this feast and all the days of our lives, now and for ever. Amen.
[Today] the Lord Jesus, the king of glory, the conqueror of sin and death, ascended to heaven while the angels sang his praises (Eucharistic Prayer, Ascension I).	O mighty God, the heavenly and earthly creatures proclaim you as their Lord; the far corners of the earth exalt you as their Creator and Savior. You came to us from your Father's house to draw us

Roman Rite	Maronite Rite
	close to you. You enable us to inherit the heavenly kingdom, though we are not worthy of an inheritance on earth. In your ascension, you achieved your marvelous plan of salvation and perfected all the mysteries prefigured by the prophets. One prophet announced of you: God the Lord ascended in glory, with blasts of trumpets! Another prophet envisioned you as a Lord sitting on a majestic throne, while the angels surrounded him, shouting: Holy, holy is the Lord of hosts! A third one wondered: Who is this man coming from the country of Edom, his clothes soaked with blood? Others contemplated you standing on the shoulders of the cherubim, and on the wings of the Spirit. One prophet foresaw you rising from death; and another heralded you as a glorious and mighty Lord. One prophet imagined your coming on the clouds, and another your ascension to the heights, taking a host of captives and giving gifts to people. Another prophet chanted to you, saying: God said to my Lord, "Sit on my right, and I will make of your enemies a footstool."

Roman Rite	Maronite Rite
Christ, the mediator between God and man, judge of the world and Lord of all, has passed beyond our sight, not to abandon us but to be our hope. Christ is the beginning, the head of the Church; where he has gone, we hope to follow (Eucharistic Prayer, Ascension I).	Now, O Lord, on this day of your ascension to your Sender, we implore you with the fragrance of this incense: lift up our souls and minds along with you, free them from the vanities of this world and guide them to the understanding of your divine truth. Enlighten our thoughts and consciences with the radiance of your ineffable love, raise us in the company of the spiritual hosts and prepare us for your eternal and great feast. Forgive us in your mercy and grant us to overcome temptation. Strengthen us to abide by your holy commandments. Lead us to a good end that pleases you. Grant peace to all the faithful departed who, with true faith, have slept in your hope. We will offer you glory and thanksgiving, now and for ever (Hoosoyo, Prayer of Forgiveness, Feast of the Ascension).

Summary

From reading these rich liturgical texts, we once again find that the truths of our faith discussed in the *Catechism of the Catholic Church*, this time about Jesus the Son of God, are reflected in liturgical tradition without losing any of their theological depth. Once again we find these liturgical prayers address the threefold question of who God is, who we are, and who we ought to be, and do so in a much easier way to follow than the texts of the *Catechism*. Because of their simplicity, the liturgical texts are well able to serve the faithful in everyday life. The liturgical texts can be compared with the catechetical texts; they can be meditated upon and prayed as a source of life and light for becoming liturgical people who, encountering Jesus Christ the Son of God, become sons and daughters of the resurrection.

Eight

God the Holy Spirit

In this chapter we will compare the presentation of the Holy Spirit in the *Catechism of the Catholic Church* and in the liturgy.

God the Holy Spirit in the *Catechism of the Catholic Church*

The *Catechism of the Catholic Church* reminds us of the Holy Spirit, Giver of Divine Life. This Spirit is the Lord who gives life. In the beginning, he hovered over creation and revealed God's goodness through what he created, in particular through man, created in his image, making him sharer in the divine life.

> *The Spirit is part of the beginning of all creatures*
>
> 703 The Word of God and his Breath are at the origin of the being and life of every creature....
>
> *Through the work of the Holy Spirit we are designed*
>
> 704 "God fashioned man with his own hands [that is, the Son and the Holy Spirit] and impressed his own form on the flesh he had fashioned....

This Spirit, even before Christ's coming, prepares the plan of salvation and the redeeming work (see #706 previously cited). This Spirit enlightens judges, consecrates kings, and inspires prophets. But for him to dwell in man, man first needed reconciliation with God.

Like Jesus, the Spirit was always working, though hidden

702 From the beginning until "the fullness of time"...the joint mission of the Father's Word and Spirit remains *hidden*, but it is at work....

Jesus would restore God's glory through the Spirit

705 ...The promise made to Abraham inaugurates the economy of salvation, at the culmination of which the Son himself will assume that "image"... and restore it in the Father's "likeness" by giving it again its Glory, the Spirit who is "the giver of life."

This Holy Spirit must rest on the Messiah—the Anointed One—who in turn will communicate to people, giving them once again the vision of God.

God's prophecy of salvation included the Spirit's coming

711 "Behold, I am doing a new thing"....Two prophetic lines were to develop, one leading to the expectation of the Messiah, the other pointing to the announcement of a new Spirit....

The Messiah was foreseen by Isaiah

712 The characteristics of the awaited *Messiah* begin to appear in the "Book of Emmanuel" ("Isaiah said this when he saw his glory,"...speaking of Christ)....

God's Spirit would be poured out at the time of the Messiah

713 The..."Servant songs"....proclaim the meaning of Jesus' Passion and show how he will pour out the Holy Spirit to give life to the many; not as an outsider, but by embracing our "form as slave."

The Good News began with Isaiah

714 This is why Christ inaugurates the proclamation of the Good News by making his own the following passage from Isaiah....

The incarnation is the work of the Holy Spirit

723 In Mary, the Holy Spirit *fulfills* the plan of the Father's loving goodness. With and through the Holy Spirit, the Virgin conceives and gives birth to the Son of God....

The Spirit revealed the Son in Mary

724 In Mary, the Holy Spirit *manifests* the Son of the Father, now become the Son of the Virgin....

The Spirit revealed Jesus as Messiah after his baptism

719 In [John the Baptist], the Holy Spirit concludes his speaking through the prophets...."He on whom you see the Spirit descend and remain, this is he who baptizes with the Holy Spirit. And I have seen and have borne witness that this is the Son of God.... Behold, the Lamb of God."

The Spirit began to restore God's image through Jesus

720 Finally, with John the Baptist, the Holy Spirit begins the restoration to man of "the divine likeness," prefiguring what he would achieve with and in Christ.

The Spirit manifested himself in important moments of Jesus' life

538 ...Driven by the Spirit into the desert, Jesus remains there for forty days without eating; he lives among wild beasts, and angels minister to him....

This Spirit is Jesus' own spirit; after the resurrection, Jesus will send him from the Father

728 Jesus does not reveal the Holy Spirit fully, until he himself has been glorified through his Death and Resurrection. Nevertheless, little by little he alludes to him....

The Spirit will teach us and lead us to truth

729 ...The Spirit will teach us everything, remind us of all that Christ said to us and bear witness to him. The Holy Spirit will lead us into all truth....

The promised Spirit gives us, through Christ, filial adoption and divine inheritance

731 On the day of Pentecost...Christ's Passover is fulfilled in the outpouring of the Holy Spirit...of his fullness, Christ, the Lord, pours out the Spirit in abundance.

The Spirit ushers the world into the yet-incomplete kingdom

732 By his coming, which never ceases, the Holy Spirit causes the world to enter into the...Kingdom already inherited though not yet consummated....

The Spirit gives us power as our inheritance

735 He, then, gives us the "pledge" or "first fruits" of our inheritance: the very life of the Holy Trinity...to love as "God [has] loved us." This love...is the source of the new life in Christ, made possible because we have received "power" from the Holy Spirit....

Through the Spirit's power, we bear fruit

536 ...The Spirit whom Jesus possessed in fullness from his conception comes to "rest on him.."...Jesus will be the source of the Spirit for all mankind....

The church is the temple of the Holy Spirit

537 Through Baptism the Christian is
sacramentally assimilated to Jesus, who in his own
baptism anticipates his death and resurrection.
The Christian must...be reborn of water and the
Spirit so as to become the Father's beloved son in
the Son and "walk in newness of life"....

God the Holy Spirit
in Liturgical Tradition

Now, after having sketched how the Holy Spirit is presented in the *Catechism of the Catholic Church*, let us explore
through liturgical texts, as we did in previous chapters, how
the same truths are expressed in the liturgy.

Roman Rite	Maronite Rite
The Spirit who comes from the Father will glorify me, alleluia (Liturgy of the Hours, Antiphon 3, Evening Prayer I, Pentecost).	If the Father is spoken of, the Son and the Spirit are with him. And if the Son is spoken of, the Father and the Spirit are known through him. And if the Spirit is spoken of, the Father and Son are perfected in him. The Father begets but is unbegotten. The Son is begotten but does not beget. And the Holy Spirit proceeds from the Father and partakes of the Son, and his essence is of the same nature as the essence of the Son.
We believe in the Holy Spirit, the Lord, the giver of life, who proceeds from the Father	May we be worthy to praise, confess and glorify the Light. He shines upon all, and his radiance

God the Holy Spirit

Roman Rite

and the Son.
  With the Father and the Son
he is worshiped and glorified.
  He has spoken through the
Prophets
(Profession of Faith, Sundays and
solemnities).

How wonderful are the works of
  the Spirit,
revealed in so many gifts!
Yet how marvelous is the unity
the Spirit creates from their
  diversity,
as he dwells in the hearts of your
  children,
filling the whole Church with his
  presence
and guiding it with his wisdom!
(Eucharistic Prayer, Christian
Unity).

Maronite Rite

never sets: He is supreme,
incomprehensible, eternal and
beyond all times. He is the Holy
Spirit who proceeds from the
Father and the Son, perfecting
the mystery of the Trinity; he is
the fount of divine gifts; he
speaks through prophets, apostles
and the whole Church; he is the
Lord, maker of life and giver of
all life, creating, supporting and
ruling all; with the Father and
Son, he fills all with his self, one
perfect Trinity from Three
Perfect Persons, yet one God
whom we recall and praise, now
and forever. Amen.

O God, Spirit Paraclete, in the
past, you spoke through the
prophets, and in recent times
through the apostles. You are the
sanctifier of the Churches, the
achiever of divine services, the
bestower of holy orders, the
perfecter of baptism, the purifier
of mysteries, the forgiver of sins.
You are the power from whom
flows all strength to your servants.
You are the clear Spirit who
reveals the mysterious depths of
the Father and the Son; who
manifests the secrets and old
things. You are the Spirit, wonder
maker; the Spirit who is partaken,
but does not partake; who

164

Roman Rite

Maronite Rite

perfects, but is not perfected; who
fulfills, but is not fulfilled; who
sanctifies; but is not sanctified;
who deifies, but is not deified.
You are the fount of grace, the
Spirit who calls his children to
holy orders. You are the Spirit of
Truth, wisdom, knowledge, piety,
guidance and consolation. You
are the Spirit who builds temples
for himself and distributes his
grace to all. You are the royal
Spirit; the good Spirit; the Spirit
of fortitude and might; the Spirit
of perfection; the simple and
absolute Spirit. You are the Spirit,
lover of all people. You perfect
the prophets and apostles, sustain
the martyrs, adorn the temples,
bring forth the doctrine to the
teachers and grant wisdom to the
simple. You are the Spirit
benefactor and the omnipotent
Spirit. Through you, the Son is
believed and the Father revealed,
and with you they are both
worshiped.

By the light of your Spirit,
enlighten the world and dispel
the darkness of our times, turn
hatred into love, sorrow into joy,
and war into the peace we so
desire (Liturgy of the Hours,
Intercessions, Evening Prayer I,
Pentecost).

Therefore, O God, Spirit
Paraclete, we implore you with
the fragrance of this incense:
send upon us your spiritual gifts;
fill us with the wisdom of your
teachings; make us temples for
your honor; inebriate us with the
wine of your grace; adorn us with

Roman Rite

Maronite Rite

the touch of your blessings; shine upon us your radiant light. O God, Spirit Paraclete, grant us to find peace in you. Let us worship you in purity and holiness, and with your assistance, worship the hidden Father and the adored Son, from whom you proceed, one ineffable, incomprehensible and invisible God, now and for ever. Amen (Hoosoyo,Prayer of Forgiveness, Feast of Pentecost, Maronite Liturgy).

God of power and mercy,
send your Holy Spirit
to live in our hearts
and make us temples of his glory
(Opening Prayer, Tuesday of the
Seventh Week of Easter).

O Lord, on the day of the descent of the Paraclete, the Comforter, give us faultless justice, so that having received his heavenly gifts we may cast off the old man completely. We shall become pure dwelling places for your divinity, advance in good deeds throughout our lives, and carry your name before all with pride. You live and reign with the Father and the Holy Spirit, now and for ever (First Prayer of Ramsho, Evening Prayer).

Father,...
Keep within us the vigor of your
Spirit
and protect the gifts you have
given to your Church
(Prayer after Communion,
Pentecost).

Father, we always give you thanks for your mercy and love, but especially on this day when you poured out, and continue to pour out, your Spirit on your children, whom you created in your image and likeness.

Roman Rite

Today we celebrate the great
  beginning of your Church
when the Holy Spirit made known
  to all peoples the one true God,
and created from the many
  languages of man
one voice to profess one faith
(Eucharistic Prayer, Pentecost).

May that fire which hovered over
  the disciples
as tongues of flame
burn out all evil from your hearts
and make them glow with pure
  light
(Solemn Blessing, Pentecost).

Maronite Rite

Today the Consoling Spirit came
upon the frightened apostles; the
tongues of fire rested upon
them,and inflamed them with an
ardent apostolic zeal. Today the
Master sent the Spirit of truth
who gives witness to him. The
disciples received the strength of
the Spirit, and witnessed to him
in Jerusalem, throughout Judea,
Samaria and to the ends of the
earth. Today they heard a sound
coming from heaven; tongues
seeming to be divided and fixed
themselves on each of those
gathered in the upper room.
They were all filled with the Holy
Spirit, the Spirit of life, who
speaks through the prophets and
apostles. He is one in substance
with the Father and the Son, the
Spirit of truth who settled upon
Christ in the Jordan. He forms
the catholic and apostolic Church
and gives it life.

And now we beg you, O Holy
Spirit, Spirit of strength,
knowledge and fear, Spirit of
Wisdom, understanding,
compassion and true love:
sanctify us, body and soul, and we
shall be resplendent and spotless
sheep. Heal us of our egotism
and enkindle in us the fire of
your love; implant in our spirits

Roman Rite

Maronite Rite

the true faith of the apostles; place within our hearts that good hope and strong consolation which will raise us above the vanities of this world. Do not allow us to live with anything that might alienate us from you and the holiness of your love: enmity, envy and hatred. Pour out upon us your gifts, the bearers of life, as you did upon the apostles. Wherever we may be, we shall confidently bear witness by our lives: in our leisure and our work, in our thoughts and words, and by the whole demeanor of our lives through the day and night. Give us your true life in this world, and in the world to come we shall glorify you by our deeds, and praise you with the Father and the Son, the life-giving Trinity, for ever. Amen (Hoosoyo, Prayer of Forgiveness, of Ramsho, Evening Prayer, Pentecost).

You gave your Spirit to the apostles, with the power to forgive sins, destroy all sin in the world. You promised us the Holy Spirit, to teach us all things and remind us of all you had said, send us your Spirit to enlighten our minds in faith. You promised to send the Spirit of truth, to bear witness to yourself, send forth

O Holy Spirit, you give holiness to the saints and wisdom to simple hearts, you came down upon the apostles and gave them strength to bear witness. Receive and sanctify these prayers which we offer you with our incense. Grant us to walk according to your gifts, the givers of life, without fear and blame. Then we

Roman Rite

Maronite Rite

your Spirit to make us faithful witnesses (Liturgy of the Hours, Intercessions, Evening Prayer II, Pentecost).

shall belong to your dwelling places, carry your name, and announce your salvation. The world shall live by you and glorify the consubstantial Trinity, now and for ever. Amen (Etro, Prayer of Incense, Ramsho, Evening Prayer, Pentecost).

Today we celebrate the feast of Pentecost, alleluia; on this day the Holy Spirit appeared before the apostles in tongues of fire and gave them his spiritual gifts (Liturgy of the Hours, Canticle of Mary, Evening Prayer II, Pentecost).

Praise, glory and honor to the only and hidden Father, to the Son, who is the Savior of all and whom we see and adore, to the Holy Spirit, who gives us life, has spoken through the prophets and apostles, and came down upon the disciples in the upper room at Jerusalem. To the Good One is due glory and honor this morning, and all the days of our lives, now and for ever. Amen.

God inspired speech in different
   tongues
to proclaim one faith.
May he strengthen your faith
and fulfill your hope to see him
   face to face
(Solemn Blessing, Pentecost).

Christ our God, when you gloriously ascended to your heavenly Father, you raised your pure hands and poured your blessings upon your holy apostles, saying: "Wait for that which the Father has promised and do not leave Jerusalem." On the day of Pentecost, when they were all gathered in one place, there was sudden sound that came from heaven; the Spirit filled them with his astonishing gifts! These simple men spoke the languages

Roman Rite	Maronite Rite

| | of the learned; these fishermen began to teach the educated. They then began to perform miracles and traveled throughout the world, preaching to the poor the Son of God who died, rose from the dead and gave us salvation. Their light spreads throughout the universe, the Spirit opens their mouths and became fishers of men. They do not fear the governors, nor do they dread death. In all places they proclaim: "God has truly manifested himself to men, and we have seen his glory." Their zeal made them seem as people drunk with wine, while it was the love of God which has been poured into their hearts, in the upper room on the day of Pentecost in Jerusalem. |
| Send into the Church the Spirit of unity, to remove all dissension, hatred and division....You prayed, and were led by the Spirit to begin your ministry, may priests find in prayer the guidance of the Spirit to perform their duties. May your Spirit guide all in authority, to seek the common good (Liturgy of the Hours, Intercessions, Evening Prayer, Seventh Week of Easter). | And now, Christ our God, we beg you always to adorn us with your Holy Spirit and marvelous gifts. Confirm us in the Catholic faith and in the universal and apostolic Church, headed by the holy Roman Pontiff, guided by our Patriarch and bishops, tended by priests, and served by the deacons. Lord, be a rampart of protection for your Church against all human egotism and vain glory. Sanctify her shepherds |

Roman Rite	Maronite Rite
	and purify her children, then we will truly serve you without being interrupted by human bias or worldly considerations.
See your people gathered in prayer, open to receive the Spirit's flame. May it come to rest in our hearts and disperse the divisions of word and tongue (Alternative Opening Prayer, Vigil of Pentecost).	O Lord, may your light shine on all hearts thanks to those who have been clothed by you in the waters of baptism, and have received you at the holy altar. Enkindle in us the apostolic zeal to carry your love to all, that they may know that they are brothers and sisters and glorify the Father in heaven. On this blessed day, grant us to receive the grace of the consoling Spirit, the bearer of life, who is one in being with you and the Father, to whom is due glory and honor, now and for ever. Amen (Hoosoyo, Prayer of Forgiveness, of Safro, Morning Prayer, Feast of Pentecost).

Summary

Yet again we can see how in these liturgical texts about the Holy Spirit the same truths are expressed as in the *Catechism of the Catholic Church* but in a simple way that touches the heart, even of those unfamiliar with scholarly methods. Each of these prayers contains a lesson that explains and prepares for the proclamation of the Word, placing it at the reach of every worshiper.

Nine

Morality, Sacraments, and Mary

Through this view of what the church believes as presented in the *Catechism of the Catholic Church* and how this belief is nourished with prayer as in the liturgical texts, we experience the foretaste of the glory to come.

The experience of the transfiguration transforms us from being passive admirers wishing to put up three tents for Moses, Elijah, and Jesus into allowing ourselves to be taken into the single tent of the Spirit. Transported into the mysterious cloud uniting us to the Trinity, we are invited to actively live out the dignity of our vocation. There we learn how to nourish it throughout our journey in celebration of the sacraments or mysteries.

Is it merely coincidence that the signing of the encyclical *Veritatis Splendor*, which details and completes the message of the *Catechism of the Catholic Church*, would occur on the Feast of the Transfiguration, or was it intended to emphasize the connection?

Morality

The mysterious cloud that envelopes the disciples, uniting them with the Trinity, is the future glory and kingdom already present. The Law, then, becomes the structure of the life of the kingdom. First given by Moses, completed by Christ, the Law leads people to the mystery of God as they live their human dignity.

> *Human dignity bestowed at creation is fulfilled in vocation*
>
> 1700 The dignity of the human person is rooted in his creation in the image and likeness of God...; it is fulfilled in his vocation to divine beatitude....It is essential to a human being freely to direct himself to this fulfillment....By his deliberate actions..., the human person does, or does not, conform to the good promised by God and attested by moral conscience....
>
> *Our divine likeness has been restored by Christ*
>
> 1701 "Christ,...in the very revelation of the mystery of the Father and of his love, makes man fully manifest to himself and brings to light his exalted vocation."... It is in Christ...that the divine image, disfigured in man by the first sin, has been restored....
>
> *Belief in Christ makes us children of God*
>
> 1709 He who believes in Christ becomes a son of God. This filial adoption transforms him by giving him the ability to follow the example of Christ....
>
> *We are to show God's image and take on Christ's likeness*
>
> 1877 The vocation of humanity is to show forth the image of God and to be transformed into the image of the Father's only Son....

Created free but affected by Adam's sin, people can take two different directions: total obedience and loving abandonment to the Father, which leads to eternal life; or total independence, which leads to death.

Moral life is to live as children of the Covenant, as children of the resurrection, as children who have left the land of slavery (Ex 20:2; Dt 5:6). Christ stands for us as an example of obedience to the Law but also of rejection when it becomes attached to externals. He presents himself as the one who came to achieve the Law (Mt 5:17-19), which he makes the Law of the Spirit (Ez 36:27; Rom 8:2), the Law of the love of God and neighbor (Rom 13:8-10; Gal 5:13-14). He becomes once and for all the paschal and eternal mystery, giving us the foretaste of eternal glory. Even so, salvation remains in a way a journey of hope (Rom 8:24) that needs to transform us and the whole world (Rom 8:23; 1 Cor 15:24-27).

The church remains, then, a sign of the kingdom to come, preaching and living the evangelical virtues, awaiting the coming of Christ in glory. The church will continue to descend the mountain of the transfiguration to live the paschal mystery of death and resurrection following in the footsteps of the master, en route to the ultimate Pasch of both church and cosmos (2 Pt 3:10).

Sacraments or Mysteries

From considering our need for moral life, it is easier to understand our need for the sacraments or mysteries in our journey, for they are Christ's action of presence in his church. They are the celebration of the Christian mystery through the liturgy. That is why the *Catechism of the Catholic Church* explains what the liturgy is all about before presenting the church's sacramental life.

The Creed is our confession of the plan of God's mystery

1066 In the Symbol of the faith the Church confesses the mystery of the Holy Trinity and of the plan of God's "good pleasure" for all creation: the Father accomplishes the "mystery of his will" by giving his beloved Son and his Holy Spirit for the salvation of the world and for the glory of his name....

God's work in the Old Testament prefaced Christ's in the New

1067 "The wonderful works of God among the people of the Old Testament were but a prelude to the work of Christ the Lord in redeeming mankind and giving perfect glory to God."...

The liturgy helps us express Christ's mystery in our lives

1068 It is this mystery of Christ that the Church proclaims and celebrates in her liturgy so that the faithful may live from it and bear witness to it in the world....

In liturgy we are united to God's work of redemption

1069 ...Through the liturgy Christ, our redeemer and high priest, continues the work of our redemption in, with, and through his Church.

Liturgy is not just worship but evangelization

1070 In the New Testament the word "liturgy" refers not only to the celebration of divine worship but also to the proclamation of the Gospel and to active charity....

The liturgy is the source of life

1072 "The sacred liturgy does not exhaust the entire activity of the Church": it must be preceded by evangelization, faith, and conversion. It can then produce its fruits in the lives of the faithful: new life in the Spirit, involvement in the mission of the Church, and service to her unity.

Christian prayer culminates in the liturgy

1073 The liturgy is also a participation in Christ's own prayer addressed to the Father in the Holy Spirit. In the liturgy, all Christian prayer finds its source and goal. Through the liturgy the inner man is rooted and grounded in "the great love

with which [the Father] loved us" in his beloved
Son....

Catechesis and liturgy are linked

1074 "The liturgy is the summit toward which the
activity of the Church is directed; it is also the font
from which all her power flows."...It is therefore
the privileged place for catechizing the People of
God....

Liturgy takes us from the seen to the unseen

1075 Liturgical catechesis aims to initiate people
into the mystery of Christ (It is "mystagogy.") by
proceeding from the visible to the invisible, from
the sign to the thing signified, from the
"sacraments" to the "mysteries."...

This is the "time of the church"

1076 ...The gift of the Spirit ushers in a new era in
the "dispensation of the mystery"—the age of the
Church, during which Christ manifests, makes
present, and communicates his work of salvation
through the liturgy of his Church, "until he
comes."...

Through the sacraments or mysteries, Christ once again
joins the Christians of all ages to make them members of his
Body. This is especially true of the Eucharist, the sacrament
par excellence that makes of us the church—that is, the
sacrament of Christ's salvation for all people.

The Eucharist is the center and the summit of our lives.
It is also the source and summit of evangelization, as the
Council of Vatican II reminds us. It is because the community
of the church, the Body of Christ, is already assembled in the
Eucharist that we can be baptized and accepted as Christ's
members.

Initiating or leading us to the eucharistic community are
the three sacraments or mysteries of baptism, confirmation/
chrismation, and reconciliation. The other three sacraments

or mysteries help diffuse the eucharistic communion in the members of Christ's Body so that the community of the church may develop and grow. Holy orders gives priests the apostolic ministry to preside at the eucharistic community of the church, serving her in confession of faith and mission as well as in celebration of the sacraments or mysteries and fraternal communion. The sacrament of marriage, called the mystery of crowning in the Maronite Rite, consecrates human love as the source of charity within the family that is Christ's Body, the church. Through the sacrament or mystery of anointing of the sick, Christ prolongs his eucharistic sacrifice in the suffering members of his Body, injecting a special strength of life, transforming them as members of his church into witnesses to the hope of the resurrection.

The Commandments and sacraments or mysteries help us walk in the company of the triune God revealed on Mount Tabor. If we enjoy the foretaste of the vision of the transfiguration as the disciples did, we will then begin to work toward our own transformation in becoming more and more fit for it. Those who have witnessed the glory of the transfiguration should have more courage to face crucifixion and keep their eyes on the hope of resurrection. By focusing our eyes on Christ, we can begin to discover our identity, as we found earlier, and begin our own transfiguration through conformity to his law. He calls us to the mountain of the transfiguration not to leave us there but to send us back down with more strength and more hope to live and preach his message.

Mary

Mary gave Jesus Christ to the world (Rv 12:5) and he became the suffering servant, but she continues to be "a great sign...in the sky" (Rv 12:1) in the suffering of birth pangs until the glorious coming of Christ is achieved in the messianic culmination (Rom 11:12). Mary is the "Ark of the Covenant" (Rv 11:19) and the woman (Rv 12:1) who fulfilled his covenant by giving to the world the King of Glory. Mary "full of grace" was the first to benefit from the redemption of her son. She is our model. Through our obedience to the Commandments and through the sacraments/mysteries, we can live out her own profound gratitude as redeemed people who will unceasingly sing her Magnificat (Lk 1:46-55).

Although Mary's place in the life of the church is beautifully treated in the *Catechism*, I will mention here only a few of the summary passages.

Mary is the culmination of redemption

508 From among the descendants of Eve, God chose the Virgin Mary to be the mother of his Son. "Full of grace," Mary is "the most excellent fruit of redemption"....

As Mother of God's Son, Mary is God's Mother

509 Mary is truly "Mother of God" since she is the mother of the eternal Son of God made man, who is God himself.

Mary is virginal

510 Mary "remained a virgin in conceiving her Son, a virgin in giving birth to him, a virgin in carrying him, a virgin in nursing him at her breast, always a virgin"....

Mary is the new Eve

511 ...She uttered her yes "in the name of all human nature"....By her obedience she became the new Eve, mother of the living.

Mary has always collaborated with her son's work

973 By pronouncing her "fiat" at the Annunciation and giving her consent to the Incarnation, Mary was already collaborating with the whole work her Son was to accomplish....

Mary was taken to heaven

974 The Most Blessed Virgin Mary, when the course of her earthly life was completed, was taken up body and soul into the glory of heaven....

Mary continues to mother the church

975 "We believe that the Holy Mother of God, the new Eve, Mother of the Church, continues in heaven to exercise her maternal role on behalf of the members of Christ"....

Morality, Sacraments or Mysteries, and Mary in Liturgical Tradition

We are reminded of the identity and dignity we are called to live as soon as we become children of God through baptism and continue to live this divine life through the Divine Life, becoming "liturgical people":

Roman Rite	**Maronite Rite**

Lord,
enlighten your chosen ones with
    the word of life.
Give them a new birth
in the waters of baptism
and make them living members
    of the Church
(Opening Prayer, Third Scrutiny,
Christian Initiation).
	O Lord, enlighten the heart of your
	servant (Name ____), who just
	received baptism. As you enabled
	him/her to become a son/daughter
	of your grace, in your merciful
	kindness keep him/her firmly in the
	ranks of your children. Grant Lord,
	that after being purified with the
	waters of your covenant, he/she
	may be a member of a royal
	priesthood, a holy nation, a
	redeemed people, a blessed
	community (baptismal ceremony).

The divine liturgy continually invites us to be journeying "liturgical people" en route to the eternal heavenly celebration:

Roman Rite	Maronite Rite

Father, we acknowledge your greatness:
all your actions show your wisdom and love....
[Your Son] was conceived through the power of the Holy Spirit,
and born of the Virgin Mary,
a man like us in all things but sin.
To the poor he proclaimed the good news of salvation,
to prisoners, freedom,
and to those in sorrow, joy.
In fulfillment of your will
he gave himself up to death;
but by rising from the dead,
he destroyed death and restored life.
And that we might live no longer for ourselves but for him,
he sent the Holy Spirit from you, Father,
as his first gift to those who believe,
to complete his work on earth
and bring us the fullness of grace (Eucharistic Prayer IV).

O Lord, glory to you who exalted all people in your goodness. The voices of heavenly and earthly creatures are joined in praise to your Trinity. In your great mercy, you sent us a Savior who appeared to us from a virgin, as a ray of light through a cloud. He took on the form of a servant while he was the likeness of your majesty. He became human, that we might be born anew from the womb of the Holy Spirit. He was our brother, and he gave us the spirit of adoption, that we might call upon you as Father. He raised us from the humble state of slaves and willed that we possess the honor of heirs (Anaphora of St. James).

You formed man in your own likeness and set him over the whole world to serve you, his creator, and to rule over all creatures. Even when he

Holy are you, King of earth and Source of life. Holy is your only-begotten Son, Jesus Christ, and holy is your Spirit who dwells in all creation. In the beginning,

Roman Rite

disobeyed you and lost your
friendship you did not abandon
him to the power of death, but
helped all men to seek and find
you. Again and again you offered
a covenant to man, and through
the prophets taught him to hope
for salvation. Father, you so loved
the world that in the fullness of
time you sent your only Son to be
our Savior.

Christ, Son of the living God, you
commanded that this
thanksgiving meal be done in
memory of you, enrich your
Church through the faithful
celebration of these mysteries
(Liturgy of the Hours,
Intercessions, Evening Prayer I,
Corpus Christi).

May He free you from all anxiety
and strengthen your hearts in his
    love.

May he enrich you with his gifts
    of faith, hope, and love,
so that what you do in this life
will bring you to the happiness
    of everlasting life.

Maronite Rite

you formed man from the earth
in your image and gave him the
joy of paradise. When he
transgressed your command, you
did not reject him, but you called
him back by the law, as a merciful
Father. You guided him by the
prophets. And when the time was
fulfilled, you sent your Son into
the world, that he might renew
your image. He became man by
the Holy Spirit and the Virgin
Mary and accomplished all things
for the salvation of our race.

May these Mysteries grant all who
receive them holiness of soul and
body, fruitfulness of good works,
and strength for your holy Church
which you founded on the rock of
faith, so that the power of evil shall
not prevail against her. Deliver her
from error and scandal until the
end of the world. Through the
mercy and love of your only Son.

O Father, keep us free from sin
and confusion. Lead us safely to
the Christian end. Gather us with
your elect, that in this divine
service, as in all things, we may
glorify and praise your most
blessed name, with that of our
Lord Jesus Christ, and your Holy
Spirit, for ever and ever
(Anaphora of St. James).

Roman Rite

May almighty God bless you,
the Father, and the Son, and the
   Holy Spirit
(Solemn Blessing,
Ordinary Time IV).

Let your Spirit come upon these
   gifts to make them holy,
so that they may become for us
the body and blood of our Lord,
   Jesus Christ
(Eucharistic Prayer II).

Lord, look upon this sacrifice
   which you have given to your
   Church;
and by your Holy Spirit, gather
   all who share this one bread
   and one cup
into the one body of Christ,
   a living sacrifice of praise
(Eucharistic Prayer IV).

Maronite Rite

(*See previous page for parallel text.*)

Make us worthy to receive these
gifts, that they may be mingled in
our souls and bodies. May they
prepare us for the blessed joy of
everlasting life, which eye has not
seen, nor ear heard, nor which
has occurred to the heart of man.
There with your saints, we will
glorify you, your Only-Begotten
Son, and your Holy Spirit, now
and for ever (Anaphora of St.
Celestine).

May he make them one Body and
Blood, one divine and holy
Mystery, so that when mingled in
our souls and bodies it will
increase the faith of all who
receive it and purify us. Through
it, may the guilty be sanctified
and evil-doers be justified. May
the angry be reconciled and the
sad know gladness. Thus, from all
and through all, glory and praise
will be to you, to your Only-
Begotten Son, and to your Holy
Spirit, now and for ever
(Anaphora of St. James).

Roman Rite	**Maronite Rite**
Through his cross and resurrection he freed us from sin and death and called us to the glory that has made us a chosen race, a royal priesthood, a holy nation, a people set apart. Everywhere we proclaim your mighty works for you have called us out of darkness into your own wonderful light (Eucharistic Prayer, Sundays in Ordinary Time I).	O Lord, let us walk the straight paths of your divine laws. Grant us to be for you a holy people, a saved gathering, and a royal priesthood. May we be worthy to rejoice with all the blessed. We will praise and exalt your most blessed name, with the name of our Lord Jesus Christ and your Holy Spirit, now and for ever.
Lord Jesus Christ, we worship you living among us in the sacrament of your body and blood. May we offer to our Father in heaven a solemn pledge of undivided love. May we offer to our brothers and sisters a life poured out in loving service of that kingdom where you live with the Father and the Holy Spirit, one God, for ever and ever (Alternative Opening Prayer, Corpus Christi).	Every time you are enriched by this divine sacrifice, I am among you. Though seated upon the throne, I am dwelling in the Bread and the cup. When you are gathered to observe this Mystery, remember my death, and proclaim my resurrection until I return (Anaphora of St. John Maron).

Roman Rite

God's holy Church rejoices that
    her children
are one with the saints in lasting
    peace.
May you come to share with them
in all the joys of our Father's
    house
(Prayer over the People, Feast of
All Saints).

Father,
you have given us the mother of
    your Son
to be our queen and mother
(Opening Prayer, Queenship of
Mary).

Maronite Rite

O Lord, may the vision of your
divine beauty be the reward of all
who come to you after living a
good life. Make us one with your
saints by whose care we have
become children of your peace
and brothers and sisters of your
only-begotten Son.

God our Father, we praise You
for the unspeakable love You
showed for us in the incarnation of
Your Son. But today we give
thanks in a special way for the
grace You visited on our poor
race by choosing Mary. You
prepared her with Your choicest
blessings to be our pride and
boast. Her holiness is beyond that
of any creature, for all were
touched by the original fall but
Mary. God chose her and
protected her from Satan's gaze.
He crowned her queen of all
creation, and among mortals she
alone was so exalted. Therefore
today all creation joins to sing her
praises and to worship the One
Who filled her with His gifts. To
Him is due glory, for ever
(Hoosoyo, Prayer of Forgiveness,
The Immaculate Conception of
the Mother of God).

Roman Rite

Father,
you prepared the heart of the
   Virgin Mary
to be a fitting home for your Holy
   Spirit.
By her prayers
may we become a more worthy
   temple of your glory
(Opening Prayer, Immaculate
Heart of Mary).

Maronite Rite

O blessed Mother of God, lowly
virgin who received the lofty One,
dwelling place of Divinity, temple
of the Creator, tabernacle of the
Word, chamber of the Heavenly
Bridegroom, announcer of peace
to our race, you are the glory and
boast of all the faithful! From
earliest times you were depicted
symbolically by the prophets. You
are the ark of Noah, the offering
of Melchizedech, the field of
Isaac, the ladder of Jacob, the
vessel of manna and the rock of
Samuel. All the generations of
earth call you blessed and exalt
the One Who appeared from you.
Into your hands we entrust our
prayers and petitions. Place them
at the feet of the Child of our
hope, your Son of compassion.
May we have cause to celebrate
throughout life's pilgrimage, and
may the joy of His holy birth
sustain us on our journey. To
Him are due glory and honor,
now and forever (Sedro, Praises of
the Mother of God).

We exalt you, virgin Mother of
God, fleece that absorbed the dew
of heaven, blessed field of grain
to satisfy the hunger of creation.
You are the holy mountain from
which the Rock was hewn, without

Roman Rite	Maronite Rite
	human hands. The generations of heaven and earth join to say:

Maronite Rite

human hands. The generations of
heaven and earth join to say:

Blessed are you,
 ark of Mysteries,
Blessed are you,
 altar of the First Fruit.
Blessed are you,
 fertile valley.
Blessed are you,
 bright sunrise.
Blessed are you,
 joy of motherhood.

We petition You, O Christ,
through the prayers of Your holy
Mother. Renew the face of the
earth which You created out of
love for us. Where there is death
and decay, restore life; where
there is famine and suffering,
bring relief; where the earth is
parched and unyielding, provide
rain. Bless the fields with grain,
the fruit trees with blossoms and
the bushes with new growth.
Restore the work of Your hands,
so that earth and all that is on it
may worship You, now and for
ever (Sedro, Our Lady of the
Seeds, Patroness of Planting).

Summary

As children of the resurrection, we like Christ obey the Law not according to externals but rather living its spirit that he completed as he became the eternal paschal mystery that feeds us on our journey, sanctifying us and helping us sanctify the world. Through the sacraments or mysteries, he joins us on our journey and he becomes the center of our life, making us eucharistic people. Mary stands always as our model.

Ten

The Transfiguration and the Catechist

In the first chapter, we looked at the transfiguration event and deduced some catechetical principles. We then reviewed the history of catechesis from its beginning through the *Catechism of the Catholic Church*, spending the major part of the book highlighting the main themes of the *Catechism* and parallel liturgical texts that could help the faithful become living catechisms (liturgical people). In this last chapter, we will try to develop how the catechist or teacher can bring these principles to life.

The modern world is filled with new inventions that are always presented as sources of new hope, from Oil of Olay that keeps you forever young to the rejuvenation of the brain that should bring a long, happy life. But the more this world is filled with these inventions, the more the human heart becomes filled with things; and the more our hearts are filled with things, the more empty they become than ever. What should be sources of satisfaction become sources of complaint, not only to the average Christian but still more to catechists and teachers, who feel an even deeper emptiness because of their more refined spiritual life.

If we remain on the level of complaint, the more the pain of emptiness invades us. The only solution is to switch from the level of complaint to the level of commitment. In the transfiguration event, commitment finds its source of strength, for it is on Mount Tabor that Jesus wished to tell us of his true self. Although we have seen him on earth in the flesh, he remains our guiding light from above. For this reason every Christian—particularly every teacher and catechist—is called up to the mountain. There our hearts, weighed down by the world and its many inventions, will be filled with true light and lasting hope.

The Catechist Is Called

To a High Mountain

The call of the catechist is to a high mountain so as to be able to witness the light of Jesus' transfiguration and then share that foretaste of glory with others. In the Apocalypse of Peter, an apocryphal book of the New Testament, the transfiguration is presented as occurring on the Mount of Olives rather than Mount Tabor along with not only Moses and Elijah but also all the just of the Old Testament transfigured in glory with him. There is a certain similarity between this apocryphal text and the Second Epistle of St. Peter:

> It was not by way of cleverly concocted myths that
> we taught you about the coming in power of our
> Lord Jesus Christ, for we were eyewitnesses of his
> sovereign majesty. He received glory and praise
> from God the Father when that unique declaration
> came to him out of the majestic splendor: "This is
> my beloved Son, on whom my favor rests." We
> ourselves heard this said from heaven while we
> were in his company on the holy mountain (2 Pt
> 1:16-18).

Peter continues his exhortation to the early Christians to keep their attention fixed on the prophetic message as they "would on a lamp shining in a dark place until the first streaks of dawn appear and the morning star rises in your hearts" (v

19). So too we Christians—catechists in particular—are called to a high mountain to find the Light that would shine into our obscured hearts. It is on the high mountain that the master would strengthen and enlighten our paschal faith by his light.

The classroom of Jesus becomes the mountain: "Six days later, Jesus took Peter, James, and his brother John and led them up to a high mountain by themselves" (Mt 17:1). Jesus, the catechist par excellence, is trying to lead his disciples to familiarity with his secret place, the mountain, where he often escaped to be with his Father. Mountains are referred to in most religions as places where earth touches heaven, where God walks when he visits his creatures.

We need not enter into debate about which is the mountain of the transfiguration; but it is significant that Mount Tabor is the figure of the new Mount Sinai, where Moses received the Ten Commandments. On Mount Tabor, Jesus as the New Moses became the New Law and its fulfillment.

Yet according to St. Ephrem, Jesus possessed the divine glory before his resurrection—not for only a few moments but as a permanent state. It did not radiate from Jesus' face externally, as it did from Moses' face on Sinai, but internally, from his whole body. So the transfigured Christ is at the same time the only Son of the Father and the only son of Mary, manifesting divine glory from above and from his physical state. Those who separate the two are separated from the kingdom, and those who confuse the two lose the life of Christ (SS. Ecclesiae Patrum, XXXVII, 343-354—#4,9-14).

To Pray

The transfiguration event is an invitation to come closer to the transfigured Christ and contemplate the fascinating vision of our Savior from the perspective of our daily life. Why were the three disciples chosen? This question can be explained only by the divine pedagogy that reserves this particular revelation of Christ to the particular group of people most capable of contemplating him in his divine condition as the Word of God. The others will only "hear" the Word. There is a difference between hearing the Word and making the Word ours by contemplation before later proclaiming it.

The call to the mountain to pray is not a call to simple prayer. It is rather a call to contemplative prayer, in which we allow ourselves to be taken into the mystery we cannot comprehend. For the church fathers, the role of prayer is essential on the road that ascends toward the contemplation of the transfigured Christ. Even the sleep of the disciples symbolizes the mystical sleep that comes before pure contemplation. Although that sleep is seen as a sign of weakness, here on Mount Tabor it is considered as the rest that will allow contemplation of the resurrection with perfect vigilance and attention.

This kind of prayer leading to contemplation turns into vision of divine light seen with new eyes. Like Peter, James, and John, we feel great happiness as in a dream. We feel transported close to God, forgetting the world in which we live. But this beautiful vision can last only a few moments, even though our desire is to prolong it as Peter wanted to by pitching tents. Such a request interrupts the vision and the sacred silence. Even St. Luke comments that Peter did not really know what he was saying. When we shift our attention to what is visible or material, we break in upon our contemplative prayerful atmosphere.

Although prayer and contemplation could become an escape, Christ is present to remind us of reality and to invite us to go back down the mountain to our daily lives. The transfiguration now fades into a great afterglow of hope that illuminates our lives based on service, renunciation, and charity. It becomes, then, a source of life that affects not only our individual selves but also the community and the whole universe. This time of prayer, meditation, and contemplation will help us understand God's plan of salvation and discern our own mission, so that the message and the messenger are not confused.

To Be Part of God's Plan

This mystery of the transfiguration offers to us teachers and catechists one of the richest, most fascinating images of God's plan of salvation, the dogmas of our Christian life. In the transfiguration, we see the incarnate Son of God, destined to undergo passion, suffering, and death, receiving the witness of the Old Testament prophecies. At the same time, he receives the approval of the Father and the Holy Spirit. This event also formulates and directs a call, a promise of glory to the small group of disciples who become the central part of the church.

What happened in the Jordan River happens anew on the mountain where the transfiguration takes place. The cloud that symbolizes the Holy Spirit is the only tent needed, not the three tents Peter wanted to put up, for the Father, Son, and Holy Spirit are one and the mysterious cloud is their abode. This cloud overshadows us as it did Mary, who knew how to receive as well as to give the Word of God, dedicating her whole life to his service within the plan of salvation. So the transfiguration sheds some light on the mystery of the Trinity that Christ came to reveal as the center of the kingdom of God.

This important lesson of the transfiguration is crucial to helping the disciples become stronger, preparing to carry the message to others, becoming the living image of the Messenger, making it a flame that will purify and change their lives. Why is this lesson important? It is important not only because Jesus was misunderstood by the crowds who saw him as a nationalist messiah, rejected by the authorities of the nation, but also because it can help the disciples, his students, understand that this Messiah is the same Son of Man who will ascend to Jerusalem to die and be resurrected. There is the dark side and the glorious side of the lesson.

It is as hard for us as it was for the disciples to see God's mysterious plan this way. The transfiguration becomes an effective tool to give the disciples a foretaste of this glory of the Son of Man who lives with them, to whom they should give their trust and listen, unafraid to accompany him on the road to Jerusalem and glory through the cross. This plan of God they must face includes the difficult journey with Jesus, a journey that will be explained to them later.

The disciples need to understand that this Jesus who is presented as the suffering servant is proclaimed by God as "his beloved Son." The transfiguration event thus becomes a call to place their confidence in Jesus with whom they live, and to listen every day to his message, mainly this scandalous message of glory through the cross. Who would not fear this approach? Only those who place their trust in him.

In concentrating on the catechist as led to the mountain to understand God's plan through prayer and contemplation, we have specifically dealt with the message made available to the messenger. Now let us explore how the messenger is sent back down the mountain to transmit the mysterious message experienced on high.

The Catechist Is Sent

To Be a Living Image

The transfiguration event is not a magical moment, nor is it the result of human efforts. It is rather an event in which the only one who acts is God. He is the only one who can bring hope to the final, definitive, glorious achievement, for it is realized in Jesus the living Word of God through presence at the transfiguration.

If the face is the mirror of the heart, we can see how the glow of Jesus' face (trans-figure) is caused by an internal source, usually hidden to human eyes. So for Christians in general and particularly catechists, surrounded as they are by darkness and confusion, Christ's transfiguration remains a center of light and an invitation to be his living image, on whose faces others can see the glorious message we hold in our hearts. Imagine if our students could experience him glorified in their teachers!

Timothy of Antioch reproaches Saint Peter for wanting to put up tents, warning him against the dangers of Arianism—that is, placing Jesus on the same level as Moses and Elijah (PG LXXXVI, I,264). Yet both Moses and Elijah were also called to be sent, although they are not on an equal level with Jesus. They are not the message but the messengers, called to be sent and to reflect the image of God.

Anastasius of Antioch presents the transfiguration as the seal of the initial disfiguration of the Word of God, that is, through the incarnation by becoming flesh. When the resurrection comes, the final seal will be set upon the drama of the passion (PG, LXXXIX,1361-1376, #4). Like Moses and Elijah, catechists are called to clarify the Word of God so often disfigured by many personal or collective views or attitudes, mainly in the moral realm.

To Be a Living Antenna

Timothy of Antioch compares the intercession of Moses with hands extended on the mountain with the Lord's salvific crucifixion (PG, LXXXVI,I,256). In turn, we have seen the comparison between the cross and the antenna set high on the mountain, drawing down a powerful message from above, the vertical axis (its relationship with God), and transmitting this message outward through its extended arms to the horizontal axis (the plain). For transmission to occur, the message must be carried beyond the original reception point. This is why Peter and the others needed to return, even though they would have preferred to stay with Jesus up there on the mountain. Christ's mission called them instead back down to the plain where people could hear and accept the message. This is how the kingdom of God can be established in the world, not on the solitude of the mountain.

But something remains up there on the heights—something upright with arms outspread like a cross. The cloud of glory is gone, yet one bright wave after another radiates in ever-widening circles. The thing glows so brightly that it seems it would be consumed, yet it continues to beam. And there is more than a glorious sight; there is also a glorious sound, heard perhaps even more deeply in the heart than the ear.

The task of catechists, like the disciples, is to accept that they are no longer completely at home below on the plain yet cannot return to the glorious vision above—except through alignment with this antenna anchored on top of the mountain with arms extended through even the raging storms. Although the foretaste of heavenly glory up there was exquisite, now we must beam the message down where it is most needed. People await it—and because we have received it, it is now up to us to broadcast it.

To Be a Consuming Fire

Christ wanted to manifest his glory to warn his disciples of the scandal of his coming passion as well as the persecution they themselves would meet. In this way, they would not be ashamed of the cross but accept it with strong, confident hearts glowing in the flame that consumes but does not destroy.

Moses and Elijah both passed through this same fire unscathed. Although consumed by it, both men were active figures in their own right, talking with Jesus about his own exodus from this world. Peter seems to miss the meaning of the mysterious event taking place in front of his eyes, as we see him later misunderstanding the mystery at Gethsemane (Mk 14:40). But there are many reasons for Peter's wish to set up tents for Moses, Elijah, and Jesus. Although many of the church fathers disapprove of Peter's action, we can also see that through his request, Peter is merely expressing his joy, his ecstasy, his captivation by this celestial flame, and thus his desire to make a permanent dwelling place not only for Moses and Elijah but also—and primarily—for the transfigured Jesus.

But the response to Peter's request is both sudden and indirect: a cloud comes to cover them. It is not a direct rebuke; it is like a father turning his child's attention elsewhere to help him stop going on and on about something. Peter "was still speaking when suddenly a bright cloud overshadowed them" (Mt 17:5). The contrast is striking. The tent is made by human hands; the cloud has a celestial origin. The tent would only place those inside in darkness, while the cloud illumines and enlightens. In this way the outline of the cross began to stand out against the light enveloping Mount Tabor.

To Lead a Journey

Who would not be afraid to accept a journey to glory through the cross? Who would not fall trembling to the ground? "When they heard this the disciples fell forward on the ground overcome with fear" (Mt 17:6). Isn't this fear something we find common among people visited by God? Indeed, this is the classical religious attitude of everyone in the presence of the sacred, confronted by the celestial voice that affirms and confirms an event and calls for obedience.

But the Master, the Teacher, does not leave us there on the ground. He encourages us to follow in his footsteps, to continue the journey. "Jesus came toward them and laying his hand on them, said, 'Get up! Do not be afraid'" (Mt 17:7). Jesus helps us arise and continue the journey, but this does not mean that the event should be filed in the archives of past historical events.

Jesus the Word is transfigured and will always remain there to renew and surprise all those who hear it. His dazzling white clothes are, for St. Jerome preaching to his monastic community in Bethlehem, a symbol of the Scriptures spiritually transfigured by his glory (Ninth Scriptural Homily on Mark, 1-7 [CC LXXVIII, 477-484]). Only contemplation of the transfigured Christ allows us to see the figures of the Old Testament, Moses and Elijah, in glory and dialogue with Jesus. Except in reference to him, the two prophets would not even be on the mountain, remaining obscure personalities without announcing the passion of Christ. Without their testimony, this would be a dark and obscure journey indeed.

Perhaps in one sense, Peter was right about the need for putting up tents. We need a place to return to in order to re-encounter the transfigured Lord periodically. Thus St. Jerome shares Peter's sentiments, excusing him for asking to put up tents as places for meditation, a tent in the heart for Christ, the Law, and the Prophets. On our own journey, we would welcome such a place to return to in order to focus on Christ, the Light, rather than on the smaller lamps of earth that shed such little light and sometimes even distract us. As we go about our daily journey, only our focus on Christ, the Teacher, will allow us to see and understand the Law and the Prophets and to present this teaching as he did.

So let us arise and wend our way down the mountain of exaltation, returning to help others climb and find the Lord as we—like the disciples—have done. Because we have been up there, and because our antennae are aligned with the divine message of the transfiguration, we can say in confidence, "We have seen the Lord," and others will listen as we, with arms outstretched, transmit the message we received.

CATECHETICAL PRINCIPLES OF THE TRANSFIGURATION

1. The disciples are *called* by Jesus to *ascend*:
    a. The disciples are *called to a high mountain.*
    b. The disciples are *called to pray.*
    c. The disciples are *called to be part of God's plan.*

2. The disciples are *called to be sent back down*:
    a. The disciples are *sent to become his living image.*
    b. The disciples are *sent to become his living antennae.*
    c. The disciples are *sent to become a consuming flame.*
    d. The disciples are *sent on a journey.*

Conclusion

There is no better way to conclude these pages than to tell a story. This story has been adapted from a tale in *The Short Stories of Leo Tolstoy*.

Long ago in Russia, a shoemaker named Martin lived by himself in a tiny cellar apartment in a large city. He liked to look out of his tiny window, the only source of light he had there. It was just high enough that when he looked up he could see people walking by from the knee down.

Martin was a busy shoemaker, for he was an honest man and a fine craftsman. But the shoemaker was often lonely and sad. His wife had died young, while he was still an apprentice, leaving him with one son who died in early adolescence.

In his sorrow, Martin had sought the counsel of a holy man. "All I ask of God is that he bring my life quickly to a close," Martin told him. "I have become a man without hope."

"There is still reason for you to give yourself to God," said the holy man. "You will find the reason to live, and you will no longer grieve over your great loss."

Martin pondered the man's words. "How do I give myself to God?" he finally asked.

"That is what Christ showed us," the holy man answered. "Purchase and read the New Testament. There you will learn to live for God. Everything is to be found in the Gospels."

Deeply moved, Martin went to a store and bought a New Testament. Each night, after his work, Martin lit his lamp and read from the precious book. The more he read, the more he understood and the clearer and more joyful his heart became.

As depression left him, Martin faced each day with great anticipation. He worked long hours caring tenderly for the boots and shoes that entered his tiny shop. His night reading empowered him to do his finest work. One night Martin was reading the seventh chapter of St. Luke's Gospel. The story was about a rich Pharisee who invited the Lord to his house as a guest. While Jesus sat at the table, a sinful woman anointed his feet and bathed him with her tears. In the end Jesus absolved the woman of all her sin.

Martin put the book down and closed his eyes. He could imagine what controversy that incident had caused. Opening his eyes he looked again at the story. "Then turning toward the woman [Jesus] said to Simon, 'Do you see this woman? I entered your house, you gave me no water for my feet, but she has wet my feet with her tears and wiped them with her hair. You gave me no kiss, but from the time I came in, she has not ceased to kiss my feet. You did not anoint my head with oil, but she has anointed my feet with ointment'" (Lk 7:44-46).

Again Martin closed his eyes, wondering, "Would I have been like the Pharisee? He took care of himself but ignored his guest. And the guest was the Lord himself! If he came to me, would I have done the same? Now Martin had completely dozed off, still sitting in his chair.

"Martin!" A voice seemed to breathe in his ear. The shoemaker roused himself, half-awake. "Who's there?" he mumbled.

"Look out in the street tomorrow, Martin," the voice went on. "I will come to visit you!"

Suddenly Martin was fully awake. Was this the voice of Christ? Had he only imagined the words? Uncertain, he sat and paced for nearly an hour before he blew out the lamp and went to bed.

The next morning Martin rose before dawn, prayed, heated the stove, put on his cabbage soup, and sat down at his bench by the window to work. This morning, however, his mind was not on shoes. He wondered about the voice that he heard, or thought he heard, the night before. Though one part of him suggested that the whole incident was just a dream, another part desperately wanted the Lord to visit.

Like a schoolboy, Martin's eyes wandered out the window most of the morning. He saw familiar boots pass by in the new snow. As he did so, he saw old Stephen, the retired soldier who served as assistant janitor in the building, come out to clear away the snow. The old man struggled with every shovelful.

"He is worn out already," Martin thought when he saw Stephen lean on his shovel against the wall. "A man that old and frail has no business shoveling the heavy snow." Tapping on the window, he cried out to the old man, "Come in and get warm. I have some tea ready."

Moments later, old Stephen shuffled into Martin's tiny room, smiling gratefully. "Christ keep you. How my bones ache," said Martin's visitor.

"Don't bother wiping your feet," Martin told him. "I have to mop soon anyway." He poured two glasses of tea and offered his guest one, with a sugar cube. Without speaking the old man drank down the glass, turned it bottom up, sucked what remained of the tea through the cube, and nodded his thanks.

"Have another," Martin said, reaching for the teapot.

The old man drank this also, though not quite so quickly. As Stephen did so, Martin glanced out the window.

"Are you waiting for someone?" Stephen asked.

"Waiting? Well, yes I am, though I am rather embarrassed about it." He then told the old man of his dream. "It all began when I was reading about Jesus at the house of the Pharisee. Have you heard of the story?"

"Heard of it, yes, but I can't read."

Martin told Stephen the entire tale, and when he showed interest, told him other stories as well. When he finished, both men were silent. Finally Martin asked, "More tea?"

"I've had enough," Stephen said, rising. "Thank you for inviting me. You have fed both my body and my soul."

As the old man went outside, Martin was pleased but also a bit disappointed. It was already late morning, and Jesus had not yet come. He moved back to the workbench. He watched as other shoes passed by his window. He paced the floor impatiently.

On one of his trips to the door he saw a woman, poorly dressed, standing against the wall with her back to the wind. She had a child in her arms. She wore summer clothes and the blanket around the baby was thin and ragged. Opening the door, Martin cried out, "My good woman, it's easier to wrap the baby in here where it is warm."

In a moment, the woman was standing by the stove and telling her story. Her husband had gone off to war eight months before and hadn't been heard from since. She had worked as a cook until the baby's birth four months ago. "They laid me off," she said sadly.

"Don't you have any warm clothes?" Martin asked her.

"I sold my last shawl yesterday for twenty coins," the woman said. "We needed the food."

"Come," Martin said. He took her to his tiny closet where a woman's winter coat was hanging. "It belonged to my wife. I don't need it any more." Before she left he gave her a bowl of the cabbage soup and found a warm blanket for the baby.

When she had gone, Martin felt pleased that he had been able to assist her in some small way. But he also felt sad, for it was early afternoon. Where was Jesus?

As the afternoon wore on, Martin found it difficult to keep his mind on his work. He kept peering into the street through his tiny window and opened his door. While standing in the door midway though the afternoon, he saw an old woman carrying a basket of apples on one arm and a sack of wood chips for the fire on the other. As she stopped outside

Martin's door to shift her basket, a small boy snatched an apple from the basket and began to run off.

The old woman grabbed him by the sleeve and held on. The boy struggled to get loose, but the determined woman would not let go. Martin jumped up and ran outside without taking time to put on his coat. When he reached the pair the woman was pulling the boy's hair and he was screaming.

Martin separated the two, and taking the boy by the hand, he pleaded, "Let him go, Grandmother. Forgive and forget, for the sake of Christ."

"I'll give him something he won't forget," she shouted. "I'll take him to the police."

"For the sake of Christ," Martin pleaded, "have mercy."

In the next few moments a beautiful drama was enacted. The old woman released the boy. He apologized. After Martin talked to her about the forgiveness of the Savior, she gave the lad another apple and smiled. As she took her basket and headed home, the boy sprang forward and offered to carry the sack of wood chips. Martin moved to the door and watched the two walk down the street together.

As he went back inside, he felt good again that he had been able to help the two settle their differences. Yet he also felt sad because it was now late afternoon, and Jesus had not come.

The shoemaker put his tools away, swept the floor, and set his table. When he finished the last of the cabbage soup, Martin picked up the New Testament and sat in his chair by the lamp. He felt rather foolish for believing that Jesus had spoken to him the night before. But he opened the sacred book to the 25th chapter of St. Matthew. There he read, "Then the righteous will answer him, 'Lord, when did we see thee hungry and feed thee, or thirsty and give thee drink? And when did we see thee a stranger, and welcome thee, or naked and clothe thee? And when did we see thee sick or in prison and visit thee?' And the king will answer them, 'Truly, I say to you, as you did it to one of the least of these my brethren, you did it to me.'"

Images of old Stephen and the soldier's wife and the woman and the boy suddenly flashed across his mind. Then Martin realized that his dream had not deceived him; the Savior had truly come that day, and Martin had truly received him.

Was not Martin's reading of the New Testament the climbing to the mountain of the transfiguration? Was he not called to the mountain to see the glory of the Word of God? And was not he sent back down to do what Christ did—carry the cross of suffering that would become a glorious cross?

Is not this the vocation of the catechist—to climb the mount for the purpose of experiencing the Lord's glory through meditation and prayer—then return to help others experience this same glory? Although the call is to climb the mountain, it is also to be sent back down to those in need of finding meaning to the cross or to those who do not know how to accept it.

Do not let "falling asleep" in important events—as the disciples did on Mount Tabor and in Gethsemane—hinder your divine eucharistic liturgy from becoming a journey with the Lord. In this way you will become a "liturgical catechist" who leads students to the glory of the cross, the resurrection. In this way they will become sons and daughters of the resurrection too.